MACHINERY'S DATA SHEET SERIES

COMPILED FROM MACHINERY'S MONTHLY DATA
SHEETS AND ARRANGED WITH
EXPLANATORY NOTES

No. 19

Belt, Rope and Chain Drive

CONTENTS

In the following pages are compiled a number of concise tables and diagrams relating to pulleys, belting, rope and chain drive, carefully selected from Machinery's monthly Data Sheets, issued as supplements to the Engineering and Railway editions of Machinery since September, 1898. Additional tables are also included, which are published here for the first time.

In order to enhance the value of the tables, brief explanatory notes have been provided wherever necessary. In these notes references are made to articles which have appeared in Machinery, and to matter published in Machinery's Reference Series, giving additional information on the subject. These references will be of considerable value to readers who keep a file of past issues of Machinery, and of the Reference Series, and who wish to make a more thorough study of the subject. In a note at the foot of each table reference is made to the page on which the explanatory note relating to the table appears.

BELT, ROPE AND CHAIN DRIVE

Angular Belt Drives

On page 4 are shown a number of diagrams indicating the arrangement of pulleys for angular belt drives. These diagrams show the different positions of the pulleys for different directions of rotation of the shafts, and are applicable to shafts in any position, vertical or horizontal. The arrows indicate the direction in which the belts and pulleys run, and the notes accompanying the diagrams give the necessary explanation. [MACHINERY, June, 1902, Belt Drive for Shafts at Right Angles; November, 1909, Some Causes of Belt Failures.]

Proportions of Pulleys

On page 5, formulas are given for determining the dimensions of pulleys especially intended for single belt. The formulas, of course, may have to be modified to meet special requirements, but for general guidance they will be found useful. On pages 6 and 7, two diagrams are given for the proportioning of pulley arms for pulleys for double belt. As an example of the use of these diagrams, assume that we want to proportion the arms in a six-arm pulley of 120 inches diameter and 30 inches face. In the diagram on page 6, locate first the curve marked 120, and find the point of intersection with the horizontal line from 30 on the scale at the right-hand side of the diagram. From the point of intersection, follow a line vertically down to the bottom of the diagram, where the width of the arm at the center of the wheel is read off on the scale as 6 3/4 inches, nearly. [MACHINERY, July, 1908, Notes on High-speed Pulleys.]

Weights of Cast-iron Pulleys

On pages 8, 9 and 10, tables are given for determining the weight of cast-iron pulley rims when the mean diameter and the area of the rim section are given. For example, if the mean diameter of a pulley is 20 inches and the rim section 5 square inches, then find first the weight of the rim in pounds per square inch of rim section as given in the table opposite the mean diameter. It will be found on page 8 that for a diameter of 20 inches, the weight of the rim per square inch of rim section is 16.336 pounds. Hence, when the total rim section is 5 square inches, the total weight of the rim will be $16.336 \times 5 = 81.68$ pounds.

On page 11 a diagram is given for finding approximately the weight of cast-iron pulleys. The note at the bottom of the diagram explains its use. [MACHINERY's Reference Series No. 52, Advanced Shop Arithmetic for the Machinist, Chapter X, Specific Gravity and Weights of Bar Stock and Castings.]

Belt Velocity

On pages 12 and 13 are given two tables of the relation between pulley diameters, revolutions per minute, and belt velocity in feet per minute. For example, if a pulley is 20 inches in diameter and runs at 120 revolutions per minute, then, as found from the body of the table on page 12, the belt velocity, or the circumferential speed of the pulley rim, is 628 feet per minute. The table can, of course, be used in a reverse direction. Assume that a belt velocity of 1100 feet per minute is required with a pulley 28 inches in diameter. Then, by locating the pulley diameter in the left-hand column of the table and following the line horizontally until the belt velocity 1100 feet per minute is found, the number of revolutions per minute are located at the top

(Continued on page 32.)

ANGULAR BELT DRIVES

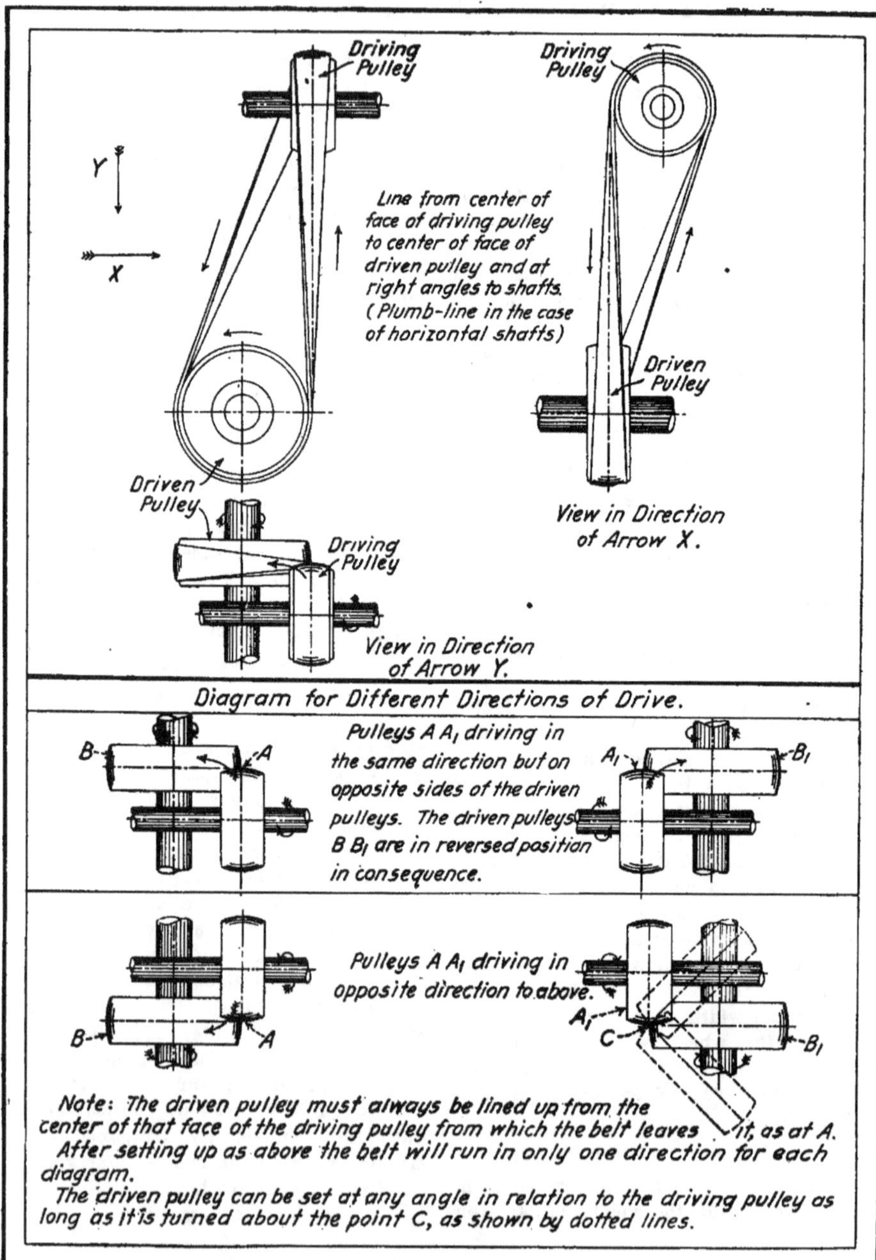

Note: The driven pulley must always be lined up from the center of that face of the driving pulley from which the belt leaves it, as at A.

After setting up as above the belt will run in only one direction for each diagram.

The driven pulley can be set at any angle in relation to the driving pulley as long as it is turned about the point C, as shown by dotted lines.

PROPORTIONS OF PULLEYS.

PULLEYS

CURVED ARM PULLEYS

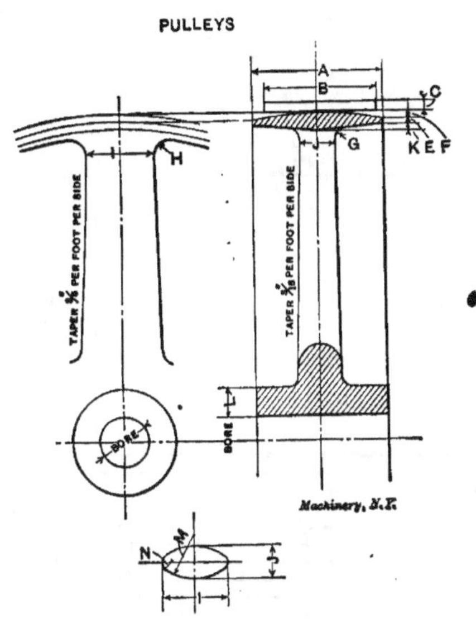

PULLEYS.

D = diameter of pulley.
A = width of face = $\frac{5}{8} \times (B + .04)$.
B = width of belt.
C = thickness of belt.
E = thickness of rim = $.7 \times C + .005 \times D$.
F = crown of face = $\frac{1}{8}$" per 12" face.
G = $\frac{1}{2}$ of J.
H = $\frac{1}{4}$ of I.
I = width of arm = $(.04 \times D) + \frac{5}{8}$.
J = thickness of arm = $\frac{1}{2}$ of I.
K = taper of rim = $\frac{1}{2}$ of E.
L = metal around bore = $\frac{7}{16}$ of bore.

ARMS.

I = width of arm.
J = thickness of arm = $\frac{1}{2}$ of I.
M = radius = $\frac{1}{4}$ of I.
N = radius = $\frac{1}{8}$ of I.

NUMBER OF ARMS IN PULLEY.

6" to 24", 4 arms.	36" to 96", 6 arms.
24" to 36", 5 arms.	16' to 24', 10 arms.
8' to 16', 8 arms.	

CURVED ARM PULLEYS.

D = diameter of pulley.
A = width of face = $\frac{5}{8} \times (B + .04)$.
B = width of belt.
C = crown of face.
E = taper of rim.
F = thickness, or rim.
G = $\frac{1}{2}$ of J.
H = $\frac{1}{4}$ of I.
I = width of arm $(04 \times D) + \frac{7}{8}$.
J = thickness of arm = $\frac{1}{2}$ of I.
K = $\frac{1}{2}$ of J.
L = $\frac{7}{16}$ of B.
N = length from O to I.
O = $I + \frac{3}{4}$" per foot of length
P = $\frac{1}{8}$ of O.
Q = $1\frac{7}{8} \times$ bore.
R = $\frac{1}{4}$ of P.
M = thickness of belt.

PROPORTIONS OF PULLEY ARMS—1

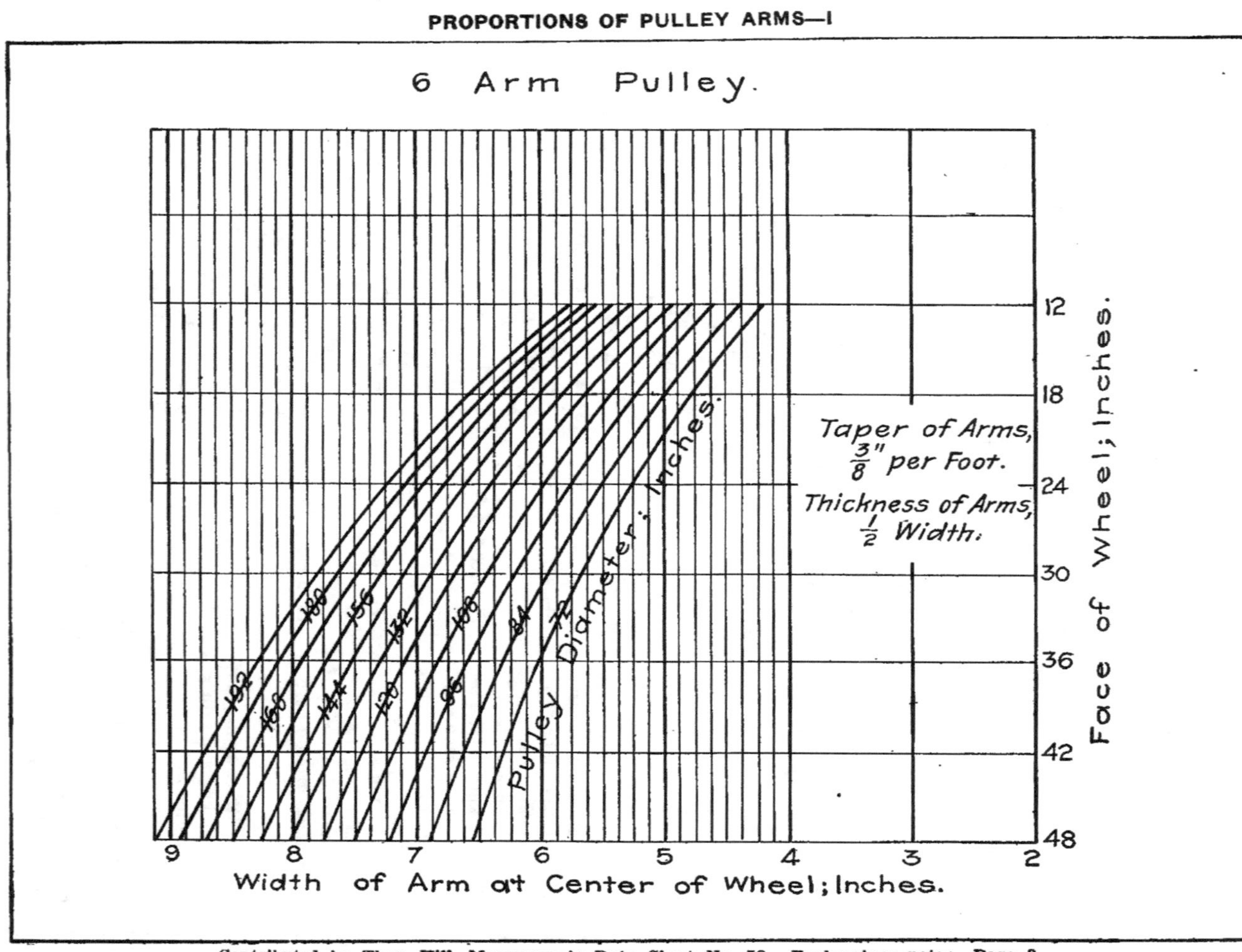

Contributed by Thos. Hill, MACHINERY'S Data Sheet No. 58. Explanatory note: Page 3.

PROPORTIONS OF PULLEY ARMS—II
8 Arm Pulley.
Face of Wheel; Inches.
Taper of Arms, 3/8" per Foot.
Thickness of Arms, 1/2 Width.
Pulley Diameter; Inches
Width of Arm in Center of Wheel; Inches.
144
156
168
192
204
216
228
240

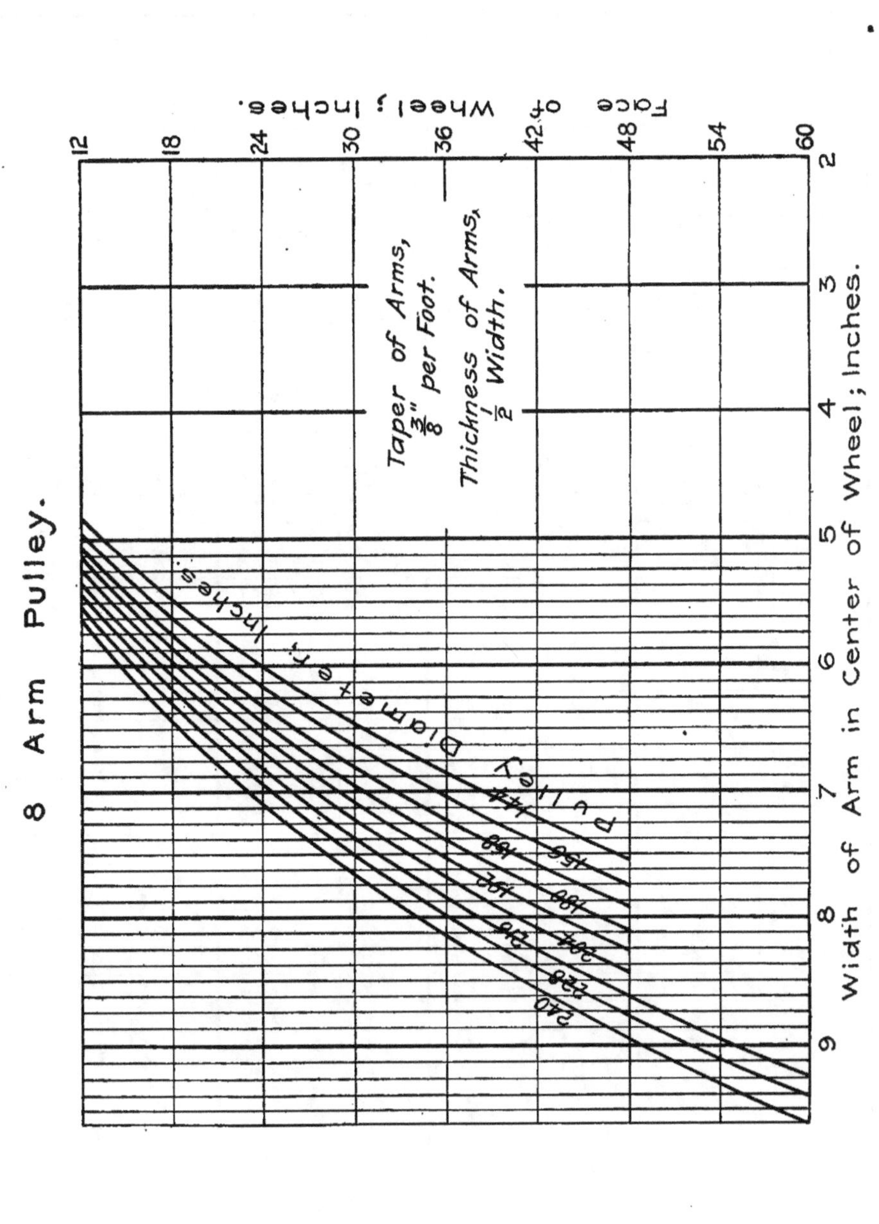

TABLE FOR CALCULATING WEIGHT OF PULLEYS—I

Mean Diameter of Rim Section

Mean Diameter of Rim Section	Weight of Rim in pounds per square inch of Rim Section	Mean Diameter of Rim Section	Weight of Rim in pounds per square inch of Rim Section	Mean Diameter of Rim Section	Weight of Rim in pounds per square inch of Rim Section	Mean Diameter of Rim Section	Weight of Rim in pounds per square inch of Rim Section
1"	0.817	2' 9"	26.955	5' 5"	53.093	8' 1"	79.232
2"	1.634	10"	27.772	6"	53.910	2"	80.048
3"	2.450	11"	28.588	7"	54.727	3"	80.865
4"	3.267	3' 0"	29.405	8"	55.543	4"	81.682
5"	4.084	1"	30.222	9"	56.360	5"	82.499
6"	4.901	2"	31.039	10"	57.177	6"	83.316
7"	5.718	3"	31.856	11"	57.994	7"	84.132
8"	6.534	4"	32.672	6' 0"	58.810	8"	84.949
9"	7.351	5"	33.489	1"	59.627	9"	85.767
10"	8.168	6"	34.306	2"	60.444	10"	86.582
11"	8.985	7"	35.123	3"	61.261	11"	87.399
12"	9.802	8"	35.940	4"	62.078	9' 0"	88.216
13"	10.618	9"	36.757	5"	62.895	1"	89.033
14"	11.435	10"	37.574	6"	63.712	2"	89.850
15"	12.252	11"	38.391	7"	64.529	3"	90.667
16"	13.069	4' 0"	39.208	8"	65.345	4"	91.484
17"	13.886	1"	40.024	9"	66.162	5"	92.301
18"	14.102	2"	40.841	10"	66.979	6"	93.118
19"	15.519	3"	41.658	11"	67.796	7"	93.934
20"	16.336	4"	42.475	7' 0"	68.613	8"	94.751
21"	17.153	5"	43.291	1"	69.429	9"	95.568
22"	17.970	6"	44.108	2"	70.246	10"	96.385
23"	18.787	7"	44.925	3"	71.063	11"	97.202
2' 0"	19.604	8"	45.742	4"	71.880	10' 0"	98.018
1"	20.421	9"	46.559	5"	72.697	1"	98.835
2"	21.237	10"	47.375	6"	73.513	2"	99.652
3"	22.054	11"	48.192	7"	74.330	3"	100.469
4"	22.871	5' 0"	49.009	8"	75.147	4"	101.286
5"	23.687	1"	49.825	9"	75.963	5"	102.102
6"	24.504	2"	50.643	10"	76.781	6"	102.919
7"	25.321	3"	51.459	11"	77.598	7"	103.736
8"	26.138	4"	52.276	8' 0"	78.415	8"	104.553

Contributed by A. B. Bramble.   Explanatory note: Page 3.

TABLE FOR CALCULATING WEIGHT OF PULLEYS—II

Mean Diameter of Rim Section	Weight of Rim in pounds per square inch of Rim Section	Mean Diameter of Rim Section	Weight of Rim in pounds per square inch of Rim Section	Mean Diameter of Rim Section	Weight of Rim in pounds per square inch of Rim Section	Mean Diameter of Rim Section	Weight of Rim in pounds per square inch of Rim Section
10'9"	105.370	14'2"	138.859	17'7"	172.348	21'0"	205.838
10"	106.186	3"	139.676	8"	173.165	1"	206.654
11"	107.003	4"	140.493	9"	173.982	2"	207.471
11'0"	107.820	5"	141.310	10"	174.799	3"	208.288
1"	108.637	6"	142.127	11"	175.616	4"	209.155
2"	109.454	7"	142.943	18'0"	176.433	5"	209.922
3"	110.270	8"	143.760	1"	177.250	6"	210.739
4"	111.087	9"	144.577	2"	178.067	7"	211.555
5"	111.904	10"	145.394	3"	178.884	8"	212.372
6"	112.721	11"	146.211	4"	179.700	9"	213.189
7"	113.538	15'0"	147.027	5"	180.517	10"	214.006
8"	114.354	1"	147.844	6"	181.334	11"	214.823
9"	115.171	2"	148.661	7"	182.151	22'0"	215.640
10"	115.988	3"	149.478	8"	182.968	1"	216.456
11"	116.805	4"	150.295	9"	183.784	2"	217.273
12'0"	117.621	5"	151.111	10"	184.601	3"	218.090
1"	118.438	6"	151.928	11"	185.418	4"	218.907
2"	119.255	7"	152.745	19'0"	186.235	5"	219.724
3"	120.072	8"	153.562	1"	187.052	6"	220.541
4"	120.889	9"	154.379	2"	187.868	7"	221.357
5"	121.706	10"	155.195	3"	188.685	8"	222.174
6"	122.522	11"	156.012	4"	189.502	9"	222.991
7"	123.339	16'0"	156.829	5"	190.319	10"	223.808
8"	124.156	1"	157.646	6"	191.156	11"	224.625
9"	124.973	2"	158.463	7"	191.952	23'0"	225.442
10"	125.790	3"	159.279	8"	192.789	1"	226.258
11"	126.607	4"	160.098	9"	193.586	2"	227.075
13'0"	127.424	5"	160.913	10"	194.403	3"	227.892
1"	128.241	6"	161.730	11"	195.220	4"	228.709
2"	129.058	7"	162.547	20'0"	196.036	5"	229.526
3"	129.875	8"	163.363	1"	196.853	6"	230.343
4"	130.691	9"	164.180	2"	197.670	7"	231.159
5"	131.508	10"	164.997	3"	198.487	8"	231.976
6"	132.325	11"	165.814	4"	199.304	9"	232.793
7"	133.142	17'0"	166.631	5"	200.120	10"	233.610
8"	133.959	1"	167.448	6"	200.937	11"	234.427
9"	134.775	2"	168.264	7"	201.754	24'0"	235.244
10"	135.592	3"	169.081	8"	202.571	1"	236.060
11"	136.409	4"	169.898	9"	203.388	2"	236.877
14'0"	137.226	5"	170.715	10"	204.204	3"	237.694
1"	138.043	6"	171.531	11"	205.020	4"	238.511

Contributed by A. B. Bramble.   Explanatory note: Page 3.

TABLE FOR CALCULATING WEIGHT OF PULLEYS—III

Mean Diameter of Rim Section	Weight of Rim in pounds per square inch of Rim Section	Mean Diameter of Rim Section	Weight of Rim in pounds per square inch of Rim Section	Mean Diameter of Rim Section	Weight of Rim in pounds per square inch of Rim Section	Mean Diameter of Rim Section	Weight of Rim in pounds per square inch of Rim Section
24'5"	239.328	27'10"	272.818	31'3"	306.308	34'8"	339.798
6"	240.145	11"	273.635	4"	307.125	9"	340.615
7"	240.961	28'0"	274.452	5"	307.943	10"	341.432
8"	241.778	1"	275.268	6"	308.759	11"	342.249
9"	242.595	2"	276.085	7"	309.576	35'0"	343.066
10"	243.412	3"	276.902	8"	310.392	1"	343.882
11"	244.229	4"	277.719	9"	311.209	2"	344.699
25'0"	245.046	5"	278.536	10"	312.026	3"	345.516
1"	245.862	6"	279.353	11"	312.843	4"	346.333
2"	246.679	7"	280.169	32'0"	313.660	5"	347.150
3"	247.496	8"	280.986	1"	314.476	6"	347.967
4"	248.313	9"	281.803	2"	315.293	7"	348.784
5"	249.130	10"	282.620	3"	316.110	8"	349.601
6"	249.947	11"	283.437	4"	316.927	9"	350.418
7"	250.763	29'0"	284.254	5"	317.744	10"	351.235
8"	251.580	1"	285.070	6"	318.561	11"	352.051
9"	252.397	2"	285.887	7"	319.377	36'0"	352.868
10"	253.214	3"	286.704	8"	320.194	1"	353.684
11"	254.031	4"	287.521	9"	321.011	2"	354.501
26'0"	254.848	5"	288.338	10"	321.828	3"	355.318
1"	255.664	6"	289.155	11"	322.645	4"	356.135
2"	256.481	7"	289.971	33'0"	323.462	5"	356.952
3"	257.298	8"	290.788	1"	324.278	6"	357.769
4"	258.115	9"	291.605	2"	325.095	7"	358.585
5"	258.992	10"	292.422	3"	325.912	8"	359.402
6"	259.749	11"	293.239	4"	326.729	9"	360.219
7"	260.565	30'0"	294.056	5"	327.546	10"	361.036
8"	261.382	1"	294.872	6"	328.363	11"	361.853
9"	262.199	2"	295.689	7"	329.179	37'0"	362.670
10"	263.016	3"	296.506	8"	329.996	1"	363.486
11"	263.833	4"	297.323	9"	330.813	2"	364.303
27'0"	264.650	5"	298.140	10"	331.630	3"	365.120
1"	265.466	6"	298.956	11"	332.447	4"	365.937
2"	266.283	7"	299.773	34'0"	333.264	5"	366.754
3"	267.100	8"	300.590	1"	334.080	6"	367.571
4"	267.917	9"	301.407	2"	334.897	7"	368.387
5"	268.734	10"	302.224	3"	335.714	8"	369.204
6"	269.552	11"	303.041	4"	336.531	9"	370.021
7"	270.368	31'0"	303.858	5"	337.348	10"	370.838
8"	271.184	1"	304.674	6"	337.165	11"	371.655
9"	272.001	2"	305.491	7"	338.981	38'0"	372.472

Contributed by A. B. Bramble.   **Explanatory note:**   Page 3.

WEIGHTS OF CAST IRON PULLEYS.

Formula:

$$Wt = (.0175\,D^{1.87} + 3)\,W + .0362\,D^2 - 2$$

D = Diameter of pulley in inches.

W = Face of pulley in inches.

Wt = Weight of pulley in pounds.

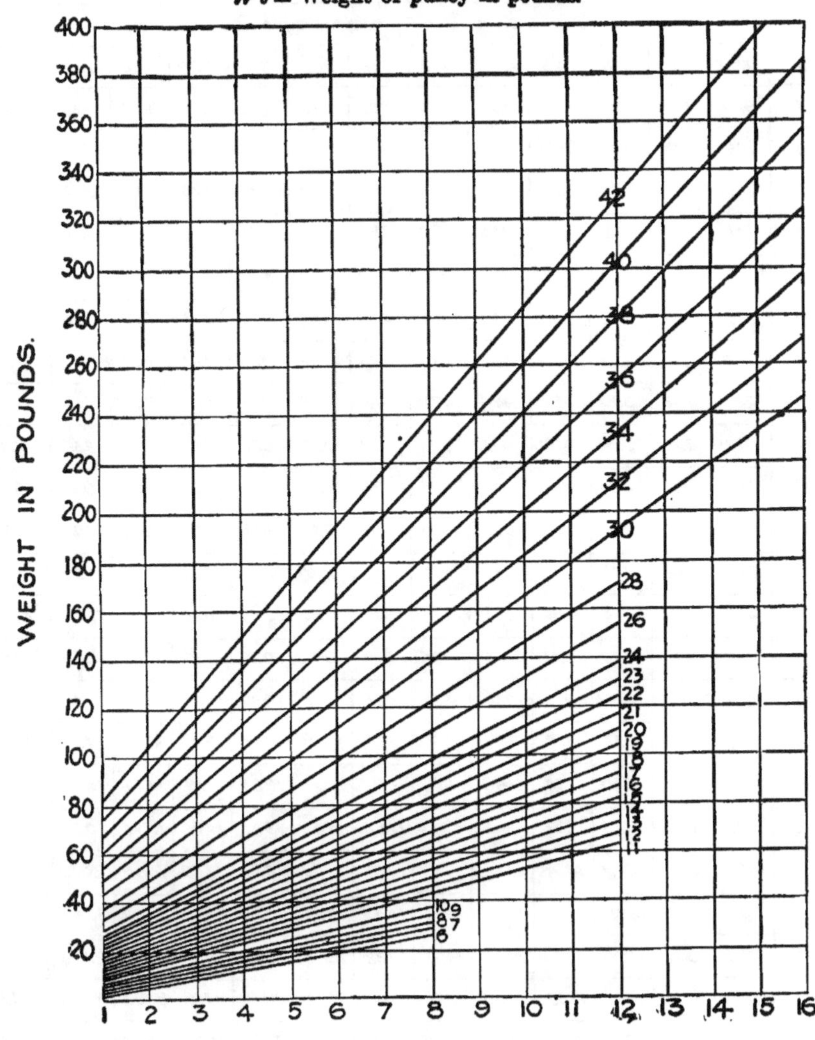

The perpendicular lines on the diagram represent the widths of the faces of the pulleys, and the diagonals the diameters—both in inches; while the horizontals give the weights in pounds. To find the weight of a pulley look for the diagonal giving its diameter and follow along this line to the perpendicular representing the face. The horizontal line at the point of intersection gives the required weight.

Contributed by Wm. Sangster, MACHINERY'S Data Sheet No. 18.   Explanatory note: Page 3.

BELT VELOCITY OR CIRCUMFERENTIAL SPEED OF PULLEYS—I

Pulley Diam. in inches	Revolutions Per Minute.												
	50	60	70	80	90	100	110	120	130	140	150	160	170
	Velocity in Feet Per Minute.												
6	78.5	94.2	110	126	141	157	173	188	204	220	235	251	267
7	91.7	110	128	146	165	183	201	220	238	256	275	293	312
8	105	126	146	167	188	210	230	251	272	293	314	335	356
9	118	141	165	188	212	236	259	282	306	330	353	377	400
10	131	157	183	209	235	262	288	314	340	366	392	419	445
12	157	188	220	252	282	314	346	377	408	440	471	502	534
14	183	220	256	293	330	366	403	440	476	513	550	586	623
16	209	251	293	335	377	419	460	502	544	586	628	670	712
18	230	282	330	377	424	471	518	565	612	659	707	754	801
20	262	314	366	419	471	524	576	628	681	733	785	838	890
22	288	345	403	460	518	576	634	691	749	806	864	921	979
24	314	377	440	502	565	628	691	754	817	880	942	1005	1068
26	340	408	476	545	622	681	749	817	885	953	1021	1089	1157
28	380	440	513	586	659	733	806	880	953	1026	1100	1173	1246
30	393	471	550	628	706	785	864	942	1022	1100	1178	1256	1335
32	419	502	586	670	754	838	921	1005	1089	1173	1257	1340	1424
34	445	534	623	712	801	890	979	1068	1157	1246	1335	1424	1513
36	471	565	659	754	848	942	1037	1131	1225	1319	1414	1508	1602
40	523	628	733	837	942	1047	1152	1256	1361	1466	1571	1675	1780
48	628	754	879	1005	1131	1257	1382	1508	1633	1759	1885	2010	2136
54	707	848	989	1131	1272	1414	1555	1696	1838	1979	2120	2262	2403
60	785	942	1099	1256	1414	1571	1728	1885	2042	2199	2356	2513	2670
66	864	1036	1209	1382	1550	1728	1900	2073	2246	2419	2592	2764	2937
72	942	1131	1319	1508	1696	1885	2073	2262	2450	2639	2827	3016	3204
78	1021	1225	1429	1633	1838	2042	2245	2450	2655	2859	3063	3267	3472
84	1099	1319	1539	1754	1978	2199	2419	2639	2859	3079	3298	3518	3738

Contributed by W. J. Phillips, MACHINERY'S Data Sheet No. 117.   Explanatory note: Page 8.

BELT VELOCITY OR CIRCUMFERENTIAL SPEED OF PULLEYS—II

Pulley Diam. in Inches.	Revolutions Per Minute.												
	180	190	200	210	220	230	240	250	260	270	280	290	300
	Velocity in Feet Per Minute.												
6	282	298	314	330	346	361	377	392	408	424	440	455	471
7	330	348	367	385	403	421	440	458	477	495	513	531	550
8	377	398	419	440	461	481	503	523	545	565	586	607	628
9	424	447	471	495	518	542	565	588	613	630	660	683	707
10	471	497	524	549	576	602	628	654	681	707	733	759	785
12	560	597	628	659	691	722	754	785	817	848	880	911	942
14	659	696	733	769	806	843	880	916	953	989	1026	1063	1100
16	754	790	838	879	921	963	1005	1046	1089	1131	1173	1214	1257
18	848	895	942	989	1037	1084	1131	1178	1225	1272	1319	1366	1414
20	942	995	1047	1099	1152	1204	1256	1309	1361	1414	1466	1518	1571
22	1037	1094	1152	1209	1267	1325	1382	1440	1497	1555	1612	1670	1728
24	1131	1194	1257	1319	1382	1445	1508	1571	1633	1696	1759	1822	1885
26	1225	1293	1361	1429	1497	1565	1633	1701	1770	1838	1906	1974	2042
28	1319	1393	1466	1539	1613	1686	1759	1832	1906	1979	2052	2126	2199
30	1413	1492	1571	1649	1728	1806	1885	1963	2042	2120	2199	2277	2356
32	1508	1592	1675	1759	1843	1927	2010	2094	2178	2252	2345	2429	2513
34	1602	1691	1780	1869	1958	2047	2136	2225	2314	2403	2492	2581	2670
36	1696	1791	1885	1978	2073	2168	2262	2326	2450	2545	2639	2733	2827
40	1885	1989	2094	2199	2304	2513	2618	2723	2827	2932	3037	3141	3246
48	2262	2387	2513	2639	2765	2890	3016	3142	3267	3393	3518	3644	3769
54	2545	2686	2827	2969	3110	3251	3393	3534	3676	3817	3959	4100	4240
60	2827	2984	3141	3298	3456	3613	3770	3927	4084	4241	4398	4555	4712
66	3110	3283	3455	3628	3801	3974	4147	4319	4492	4665	4838	5010	5183
72	3392	3581	3770	3958	4147	4335	4524	4713	4900	5059	5278	5466	5654
78	3676	3880	4084	4288	4492	4696	4900	5059	5309	5513	5717	5921	6125
84	3958	4178	4398	4618	4838	5058	5277	5497	5717	5937	6157	6377	6597

HORSEPOWER TRANSMITTED BY BELTING—1

Table Giving The Number Of Horsepower Transmitted By Belts One Inch Wide, Considering The Effects Of Centrifugal Force, So That The Tension On Belt Is Constant At All Speeds

Speed in Feet per Minute	Thickness of Belt				Speed in Feet per Minute	Thickness of Belt			
	Single	Double	Triple	Four-ply		Single	Double	Triple	Four-ply
100	0.14	0.24	0.33	0.44	3400	3.89	6.74	9.10	11.96
200	0.27	0.48	0.67	0.88	3600	4.03	6.95	9.35	12.28
300	0.41	0.73	1.00	1.32	3800	4.14	7.12	9.55	12.57
400	0.54	0.96	1.33	1.75	4000	4.24	7.26	9.70	12.73
500	0.68	1.21	1.66	2.19	4200	4.33	7.36	9.79	12.84
600	0.81	1.44	1.99	2.62	4400	4.39	7.42	9.83	12.88
700	0.95	1.68	2.31	3.05	4600	4.43	7.44	9.80	12.84
800	1.08	1.93	2.64	3.48	4800	4.45	7.42	9.72	12.71
900	1.21	2.15	2.96	3.90	5000	4.45	7.37	9.56	12.50
1000	1.34	2.38	3.28	4.32	5200	4.43	7.26	9.34	12.20
1100	1.47	2.61	3.59	4.73	5400	4.38	7.10	9.05	11.80
1200	1.60	2.85	3.90	5.14	5600	4.31	6.92	8.69	11.30
1300	1.73	3.07	4.21	5.55	5800	4.21	6.65	8.25	10.70
1400	1.86	3.30	4.51	5.94	6000	4.09	6.35	7.73	10.00
1500	1.98	3.53	4.81	6.34	6200	3.94	6.01	7.13	9.19
1600	2.10	3.73	5.10	6.72	6400	3.76	5.58	6.44	8.26
1700	2.23	3.94	5.39	7.10	6600	3.56	5.11	5.67	7.22
1800	2.34	4.15	5.67	7.47	6800	3.32	4.57	4.80	6.06
1900	2.46	4.35	5.94	7.83	7000	3.05	3.98	3.84	4.77
2000	2.58	4.56	6.21	8.18	7200	2.75	3.31	2.79	3.36
2200	2.80	4.94	6.73	8.85	7400	2.42	2.60	1.64	1.82
2400	3.01	5.30	7.21	9.51	7600	2.05	1.82	0.39	0.14
2600	3.21	5.65	7.67	10.09	7800	1.65	0.95		
2800	3.40	5.97	8.09	10.64	8000	1.21			
3000	3.58	6.25	8.47	11.14	8200	0.74			
3200	3.74	6.52	8.80	11.58	8400	0.23			

In all the above data it is assumed that the arc of contact of the belt is not less than 180 degrees.

If this arc is	90°	112½°	120°	135°	150°	157½°
Divide H.P. given by	2.21	1.72	1.6	1.4	1.24	1.17

Contributed by F. Wackerman. Explanatory note: Page 32.

The body of the table below gives the value of F in the equations:

$$H.P. = \frac{V \times W}{F}, \quad \text{and} \quad W = \frac{H.P. \times F}{V}$$

in which $H.P.$ = horsepower transmitted,

V = belt velocity in feet per minute,

W = width of belt in inches,

Example: How wide should a single belt be in order to transmit 2 H.P. at 600 feet per minute over a four-inch pulley with 140 degrees wrap?

From the table below we find that the value of F to be used under the given conditions is 1270. Inserting this and the known values in the formula for belt width we have:

$$W = \frac{2 \times 1270}{600} = 4.23 \text{ inches.}$$

Thickness of Belt	Diameter of Smallest Pulley	Arc of Contact										
		220°	210°	200°	190°	180°	170°	160°	150°	140°	130°	120°
Single	Under 8 inches	980	1010	1040	1070	1100	1140	1180	1220	1270	1330	1400
	8 inches to 36 inches	810	830	860	890	920	950	990	1040	1100	1170	1240
	Over 36 inches	730	750	770	800	830	860	890	930	980	1030	1100
Double	Under 14 inches	500	570	590	610	630	650	670	700	730	760	800
	14 inches to 60 inches	460	470	480	500	520	540	570	600	630	660	700
	Over 60 inches	420	430	440	450	470	490	510	530	560	590	630
Triple	Under 21 inches	390	400	410	420	440	460	480	500	520	540	560
	21 inches to 84 inches	320	330	340	350	370	390	410	430	450	470	490
	Over 84 inches	290	300	310	320	330	340	360	380	400	420	440

HORSEPOWER TRANSMITTED BY MANILA ROPE

Conditions assumed: Working strain $= 200 \times diameter^2$; angle of groove, $45°$; contact on smaller sheave, $165°$; coefficient of friction, 0.31.

Velocity of Rope in Feet per Minute	Diameter of Rope, inches						
	$\frac{5}{8}$	$\frac{3}{4}$	1	$1\frac{1}{4}$	$1\frac{1}{2}$	$1\frac{3}{4}$	2
1000	1.24	2.25	3.57	5.59	8.02	10.85	14.20
2000	2.70	3.84	6.84	10.68	15.39	20.93	27.36
2500	3.30	4.71	8.38	13.10	18.86	25.66	33.54
3000	3.83	5.46	9.80	15.39	21.87	29.74	38.88
3500	4.30	6.23	11.09	17.33	24.94	34.03	44.35
4000	4.74	6.83	12.15	18.98	27.33	37.17	48.59
4500	5.01	7.24	12.89	20.15	29.00	39.45	51.57
5000	5.20	7.47	13.29	20.76	29.89	40.65	53.15
5500	5.29	7.60	13.53	21.14	30.43	41.39	54.11
6000	5.08	7.32	13.10	20.36	29.32	39.77	52.12
6500	4.74	6.83	12.13	19.00	27.34	37.21	48.63
7000	4.12	5.93	10.54	16.47	23.72	32.26	42.18
7500	3.25	4.67	8.32	13.00	18.73	25.42	33.23

Explanatory note: Page 32.

PROPORTIONS OF SHEAVE WHEELS FOR IRON AND STEEL ROPES.

(Brown Hoisting & Conveying Machine Co.)

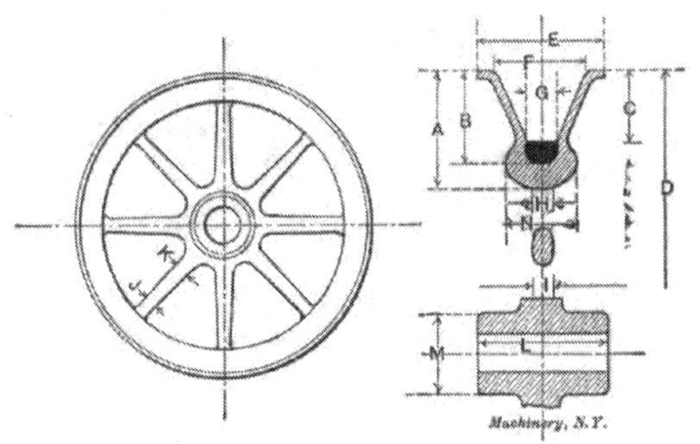

Size of Wheel	C. to C. of Rope	D	A	B	C	E	F	G	H	I	J	K	L	M	N	Amt. of Leather in Groove	Amt. of Rubber in Groove	Weight of Finished Wheel	No. of Arms
14'	14' 0"	14'10"	9½	7	5	5 13/16	5	1¼	…	…	…	…	28	…	…	…	…	5120	8 double W. I. ribs
12'	11'11"	12' 8'	7¾	6⅜	4½	6¼	5	1 15/16	…	…	…	…	20	12	3½	…	…	3442	8 straight W. I. ribs.
11'	11' 0"	11' 9¼"	8 15/16	6 5/16	4 3/16	5 7/16	4⅜	1¼	…	…	…	…	18	11	3½	…	…	……	8 straight W. I. ribs,
10'	10' 1"	10' 8"	6¼	5	3½	5⅛	4	1 5/16	1½	1⅜	3¾	5	15	12	3½	16	42	2400	8 curved elliptical.
9'	9' 1"	9' 8"	".."	5	3½	5¼	4	1 5/16	1½	1⅜	3½	4½	12½	9	3½	15	36	1800	8 straight ribbed.
8'	7'11½"	8' 8"	7	5¾	4⅛	5 7/16	4 3/16	1⅝	2¼	3	2½	3½	13	8½	3½	13	31	1390	8 curved elliptical.
7'	7' 1"	7' 8"	6	5	3½	4⅞	4	1 5/16	1⅜	1 7/16	2¼	3½	12	8	3	11	27	975	8
6'	6' 0¼"	6' 6½"	5¼	4½	3	4 5/16	3 7/16	1 5/16	1⅜	1¼	2¼	3	10½	7	3	8½	21	800	8
5'	5' 0"	5' 5"	4½	3¾	2½	3 11/16	3⅛	1½	¾	⅞	2¼	2¾	6	6	2 11/16	5½	12½	450	8
4'	4' 0"	4' 5¼"	3¼	3 1/16	2⅝	3	2 5/16	13/16	⅝	⅞	1⅝	2¼	6	4-6	1 15/16	3½	7½	275	8
3'	3' 0"	3' 3"	3¼	2¾	1½	2⅞	2	13/16	⅝	⅞	1¾	2	5½	4½	2	2½	5	101	6
30"	2' 6"	2' 8⅜"	2¾	2⅜	1 1/16	2 3/16	1¼	11/16	⅝	¾	1½	1¾	4½	4	1⅝	1¼	4½	95	6
24"	2' 0"	2' 2"	2⅜	2⅛	1	2¼	1½	11/16	⅝	⅝	1½	1¾	3½	3	1¼	1	3¾	66	5
18"	1' 6"	1' 8"	2⅝	2⅛	1	2¼	1¼	11/16	⅝	⅝	1¼	1½	3	3¼	1¾	½	1¼	46	5
36"	3' 1"	3' 5"	4⅛	3½	2	3 1/16	2¼	1⅝	1¼	1⅜	2¼	2¾	6½	5⅝	2½	4	11½	308	5
35"	2'11"	3' 2"	3½	2¾	1½	2⅞	2	13/16	¾	⅞	1¾	2	5½	4½	2	1½	5	188	6
32"	2' 8¼"	2'10¼"	3⅛	2 5/16	⅞	2	1 7/16	⅝	⅝	15/16	1⅛	2	4½	4½	1⅝	1½	4½	105	7 curved elliptical.
24"	2' 1¼"	2' 4¼"	3 7/16	2⅞	1½	3 3/16	2 7/16	¾	⅝	¾	1 3/16	1¾	4	3⅞	2	1½	4	108	6
21"	1' 9"	2' 0"	3½	2¼	1½	2⅞	2	13/16	⅝	¾	1½	1¾	4	3½	2	1	3	92	5

Contributed by S. J. Nelson, MACHINERY'S Data Sheet No. 38.   Explanatory note: Page 32.

GROOVES FOR MANILA ROPE SHEAVES

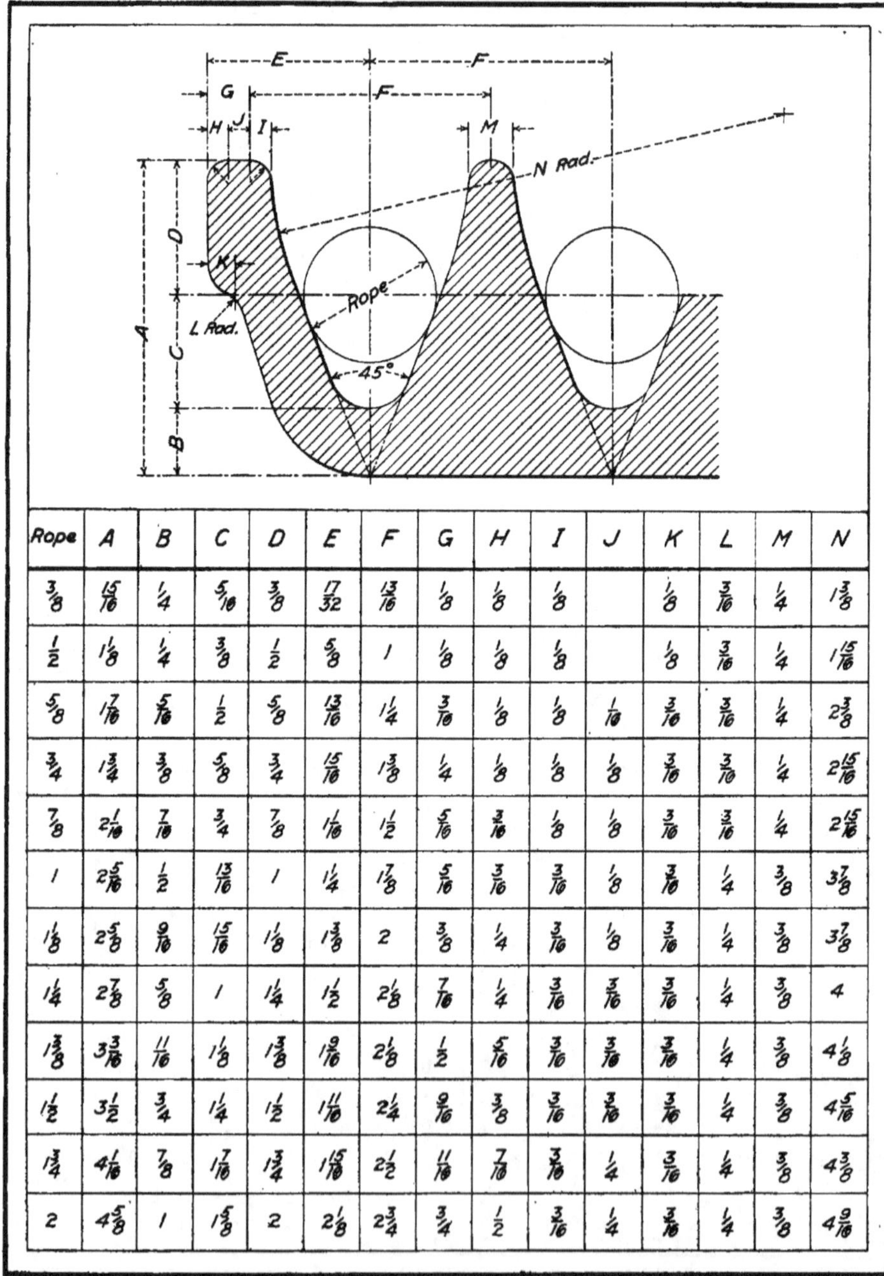

Rope	A	B	C	D	E	F	G	H	I	J	K	L	M	N
$\frac{3}{8}$	$\frac{15}{16}$	$\frac{1}{4}$	$\frac{5}{16}$	$\frac{3}{8}$	$\frac{17}{32}$	$\frac{13}{16}$	$\frac{1}{8}$	$\frac{1}{8}$	$\frac{1}{8}$		$\frac{1}{8}$	$\frac{3}{16}$	$\frac{1}{4}$	$1\frac{3}{8}$
$\frac{1}{2}$	$1\frac{1}{8}$	$\frac{1}{4}$	$\frac{3}{8}$	$\frac{1}{2}$	$\frac{5}{8}$	1	$\frac{1}{8}$	$\frac{1}{8}$	$\frac{1}{8}$		$\frac{1}{8}$	$\frac{3}{16}$	$\frac{1}{4}$	$1\frac{15}{16}$
$\frac{5}{8}$	$1\frac{7}{16}$	$\frac{5}{16}$	$\frac{1}{2}$	$\frac{5}{8}$	$\frac{13}{16}$	$1\frac{1}{4}$	$\frac{3}{16}$	$\frac{1}{8}$	$\frac{1}{8}$	$\frac{1}{16}$	$\frac{3}{16}$	$\frac{3}{16}$	$\frac{1}{4}$	$2\frac{3}{8}$
$\frac{3}{4}$	$1\frac{3}{4}$	$\frac{3}{8}$	$\frac{5}{8}$	$\frac{3}{4}$	$\frac{15}{16}$	$1\frac{3}{8}$	$\frac{1}{4}$	$\frac{1}{8}$	$\frac{1}{8}$	$\frac{1}{8}$	$\frac{3}{16}$	$\frac{3}{16}$	$\frac{1}{4}$	$2\frac{15}{16}$
$\frac{7}{8}$	$2\frac{1}{16}$	$\frac{7}{16}$	$\frac{3}{4}$	$\frac{7}{8}$	$1\frac{1}{16}$	$1\frac{1}{2}$	$\frac{5}{16}$	$\frac{3}{16}$	$\frac{1}{8}$	$\frac{1}{8}$	$\frac{3}{16}$	$\frac{3}{16}$	$\frac{1}{4}$	$2\frac{15}{16}$
1	$2\frac{5}{16}$	$\frac{1}{2}$	$\frac{13}{16}$	1	$1\frac{1}{4}$	$1\frac{7}{8}$	$\frac{5}{16}$	$\frac{3}{16}$	$\frac{3}{16}$	$\frac{1}{8}$	$\frac{3}{16}$	$\frac{1}{4}$	$\frac{3}{8}$	$3\frac{7}{8}$
$1\frac{1}{8}$	$2\frac{5}{8}$	$\frac{9}{16}$	$\frac{15}{16}$	$1\frac{1}{8}$	$1\frac{3}{8}$	2	$\frac{3}{8}$	$\frac{1}{4}$	$\frac{3}{16}$	$\frac{1}{8}$	$\frac{3}{16}$	$\frac{1}{4}$	$\frac{3}{8}$	$3\frac{7}{8}$
$1\frac{1}{4}$	$2\frac{7}{8}$	$\frac{5}{8}$	1	$1\frac{1}{4}$	$1\frac{1}{2}$	$2\frac{1}{8}$	$\frac{7}{16}$	$\frac{1}{4}$	$\frac{3}{16}$	$\frac{3}{16}$	$\frac{3}{16}$	$\frac{1}{4}$	$\frac{3}{8}$	4
$1\frac{3}{8}$	$3\frac{3}{16}$	$\frac{11}{16}$	$1\frac{1}{8}$	$1\frac{3}{8}$	$1\frac{9}{16}$	$2\frac{1}{8}$	$\frac{1}{2}$	$\frac{5}{16}$	$\frac{3}{16}$	$\frac{3}{16}$	$\frac{3}{16}$	$\frac{1}{4}$	$\frac{3}{8}$	$4\frac{1}{8}$
$1\frac{1}{2}$	$3\frac{1}{2}$	$\frac{3}{4}$	$1\frac{1}{4}$	$1\frac{1}{2}$	$1\frac{11}{16}$	$2\frac{1}{4}$	$\frac{9}{16}$	$\frac{3}{8}$	$\frac{3}{16}$	$\frac{3}{16}$	$\frac{3}{16}$	$\frac{1}{4}$	$\frac{3}{8}$	$4\frac{5}{16}$
$1\frac{3}{4}$	$4\frac{1}{16}$	$\frac{7}{8}$	$1\frac{7}{16}$	$1\frac{3}{4}$	$1\frac{15}{16}$	$2\frac{1}{2}$	$\frac{11}{16}$	$\frac{7}{16}$	$\frac{3}{16}$	$\frac{1}{4}$	$\frac{3}{16}$	$\frac{1}{4}$	$\frac{3}{8}$	$4\frac{3}{8}$
2	$4\frac{5}{8}$	1	$1\frac{5}{8}$	2	$2\frac{1}{8}$	$2\frac{3}{4}$	$\frac{3}{4}$	$\frac{1}{2}$	$\frac{3}{16}$	$\frac{1}{4}$	$\frac{3}{16}$	$\frac{1}{4}$	$\frac{3}{8}$	$4\frac{9}{16}$

Contributed by J. A. Mease.   Explanatory note: Page 32.

GROOVES FOR MANILA ROPE IDLER SHEAVES

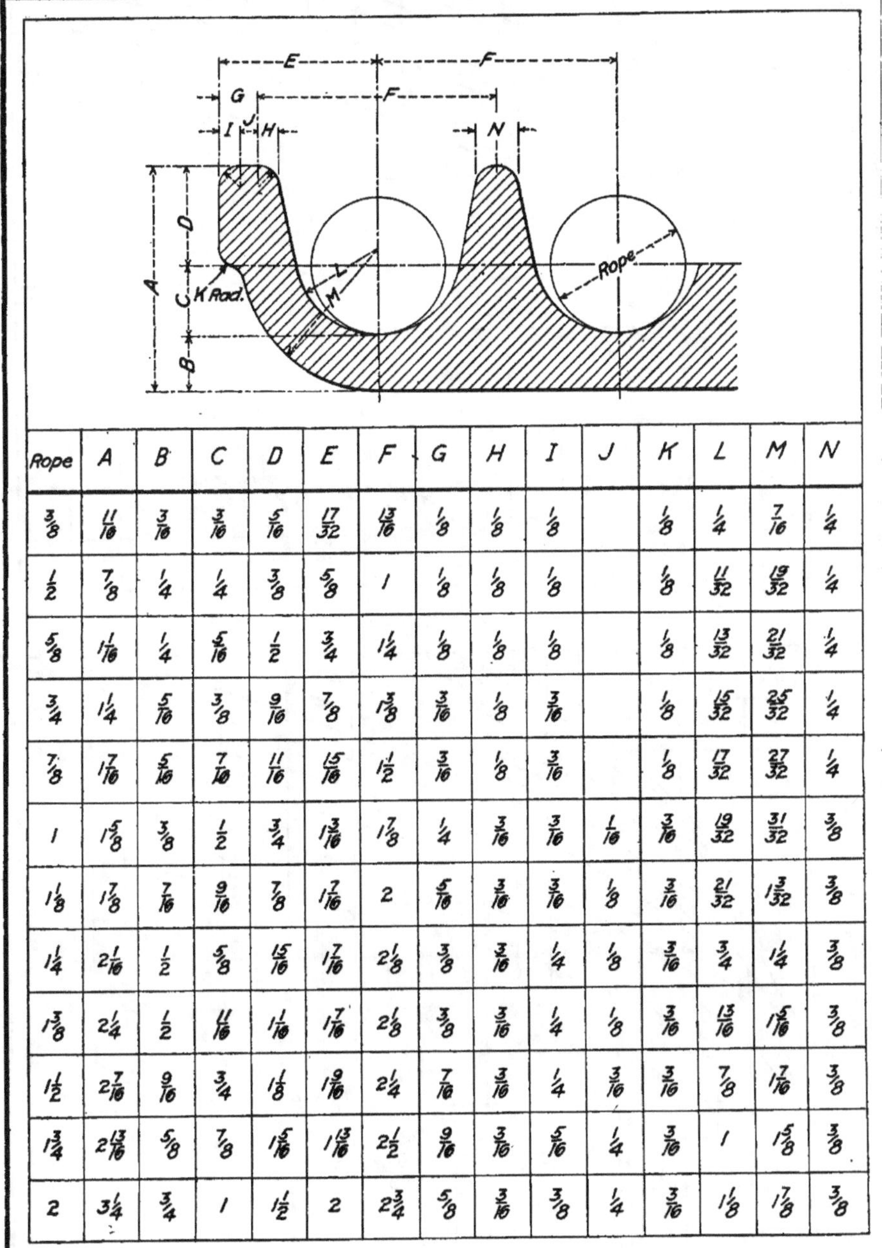

Rope	A	B	C	D	E	F	G	H	I	J	K	L	M	N
$\frac{3}{8}$	$\frac{11}{16}$	$\frac{3}{16}$	$\frac{3}{16}$	$\frac{5}{16}$	$\frac{17}{32}$	$\frac{13}{16}$	$\frac{1}{8}$	$\frac{1}{8}$	$\frac{1}{8}$		$\frac{1}{8}$	$\frac{1}{4}$	$\frac{7}{16}$	$\frac{1}{4}$
$\frac{1}{2}$	$\frac{7}{8}$	$\frac{1}{4}$	$\frac{1}{4}$	$\frac{3}{8}$	$\frac{5}{8}$	1	$\frac{1}{8}$	$\frac{1}{8}$	$\frac{1}{8}$		$\frac{1}{8}$	$\frac{11}{32}$	$\frac{19}{32}$	$\frac{1}{4}$
$\frac{5}{8}$	$1\frac{1}{16}$	$\frac{1}{4}$	$\frac{5}{16}$	$\frac{1}{2}$	$\frac{3}{4}$	$1\frac{1}{4}$	$\frac{1}{8}$	$\frac{1}{8}$	$\frac{1}{8}$		$\frac{1}{8}$	$\frac{13}{32}$	$\frac{21}{32}$	$\frac{1}{4}$
$\frac{3}{4}$	$1\frac{1}{4}$	$\frac{5}{16}$	$\frac{3}{8}$	$\frac{9}{16}$	$\frac{7}{8}$	$1\frac{3}{8}$	$\frac{3}{16}$	$\frac{1}{8}$	$\frac{3}{16}$		$\frac{1}{8}$	$\frac{15}{32}$	$\frac{25}{32}$	$\frac{1}{4}$
$\frac{7}{8}$	$1\frac{7}{16}$	$\frac{5}{16}$	$\frac{7}{16}$	$\frac{11}{16}$	$\frac{15}{16}$	$1\frac{1}{2}$	$\frac{3}{16}$	$\frac{1}{8}$	$\frac{3}{16}$		$\frac{1}{8}$	$\frac{17}{32}$	$\frac{27}{32}$	$\frac{1}{4}$
1	$1\frac{5}{8}$	$\frac{3}{8}$	$\frac{1}{2}$	$\frac{3}{4}$	$1\frac{3}{16}$	$1\frac{7}{8}$	$\frac{1}{4}$	$\frac{3}{16}$	$\frac{3}{16}$	$\frac{1}{16}$	$\frac{3}{16}$	$\frac{19}{32}$	$\frac{31}{32}$	$\frac{3}{8}$
$1\frac{1}{8}$	$1\frac{7}{8}$	$\frac{7}{16}$	$\frac{9}{16}$	$\frac{7}{8}$	$1\frac{7}{16}$	2	$\frac{5}{16}$	$\frac{3}{16}$	$\frac{3}{16}$	$\frac{1}{8}$	$\frac{3}{16}$	$\frac{21}{32}$	$1\frac{3}{32}$	$\frac{3}{8}$
$1\frac{1}{4}$	$2\frac{1}{16}$	$\frac{1}{2}$	$\frac{5}{8}$	$\frac{15}{16}$	$1\frac{7}{16}$	$2\frac{1}{8}$	$\frac{3}{8}$	$\frac{3}{16}$	$\frac{1}{4}$	$\frac{1}{8}$	$\frac{3}{16}$	$\frac{3}{4}$	$1\frac{1}{4}$	$\frac{3}{8}$
$1\frac{3}{8}$	$2\frac{1}{4}$	$\frac{1}{2}$	$\frac{11}{16}$	$1\frac{1}{16}$	$1\frac{7}{16}$	$2\frac{1}{8}$	$\frac{3}{8}$	$\frac{3}{16}$	$\frac{1}{4}$	$\frac{1}{8}$	$\frac{3}{16}$	$\frac{13}{16}$	$1\frac{5}{16}$	$\frac{3}{8}$
$1\frac{1}{2}$	$2\frac{7}{16}$	$\frac{9}{16}$	$\frac{3}{4}$	$1\frac{1}{8}$	$1\frac{9}{16}$	$2\frac{1}{4}$	$\frac{7}{16}$	$\frac{3}{16}$	$\frac{1}{4}$	$\frac{3}{16}$	$\frac{3}{16}$	$\frac{7}{8}$	$1\frac{7}{16}$	$\frac{3}{8}$
$1\frac{3}{4}$	$2\frac{13}{16}$	$\frac{5}{8}$	$\frac{7}{8}$	$1\frac{5}{16}$	$1\frac{13}{16}$	$2\frac{1}{2}$	$\frac{9}{16}$	$\frac{3}{16}$	$\frac{5}{16}$	$\frac{1}{4}$	$\frac{3}{16}$	1	$1\frac{5}{8}$	$\frac{3}{8}$
2	$3\frac{1}{4}$	$\frac{3}{4}$	1	$1\frac{1}{2}$	2	$2\frac{3}{4}$	$\frac{5}{8}$	$\frac{3}{16}$	$\frac{3}{8}$	$\frac{1}{4}$	$\frac{3}{16}$	$1\frac{1}{8}$	$1\frac{7}{8}$	$\frac{3}{8}$

BENDING STRESSES IN WIRE ROPES—I

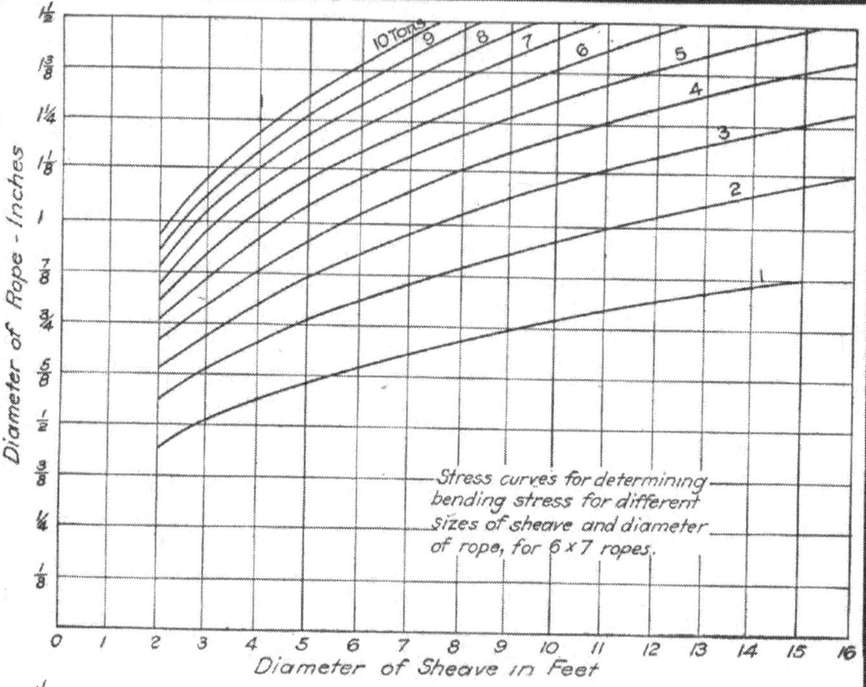

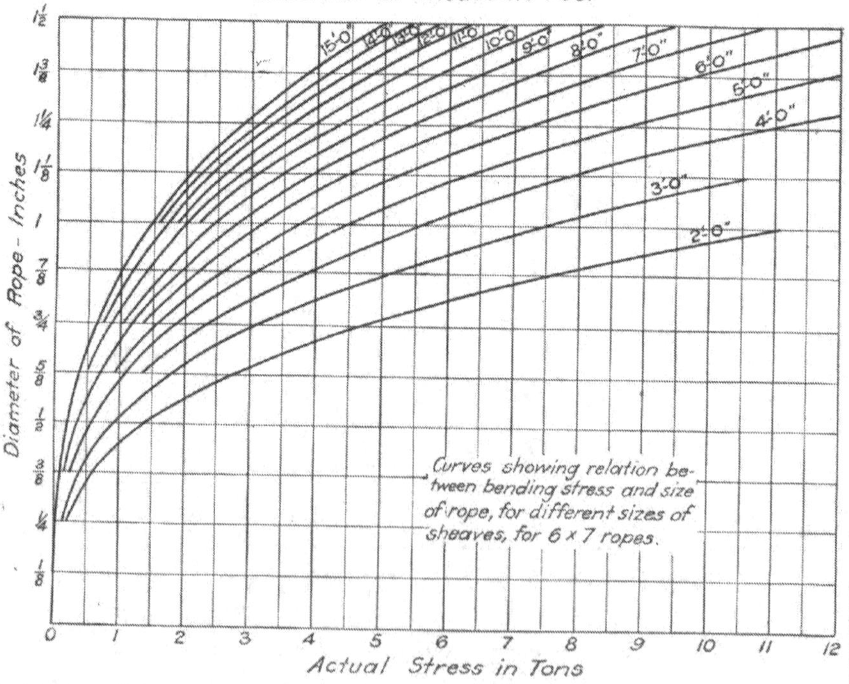

Contributed by James F. Howe, MACHINERY's Data Sheet No. 70. Explanatory note: Page 32.

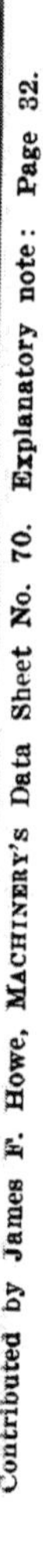

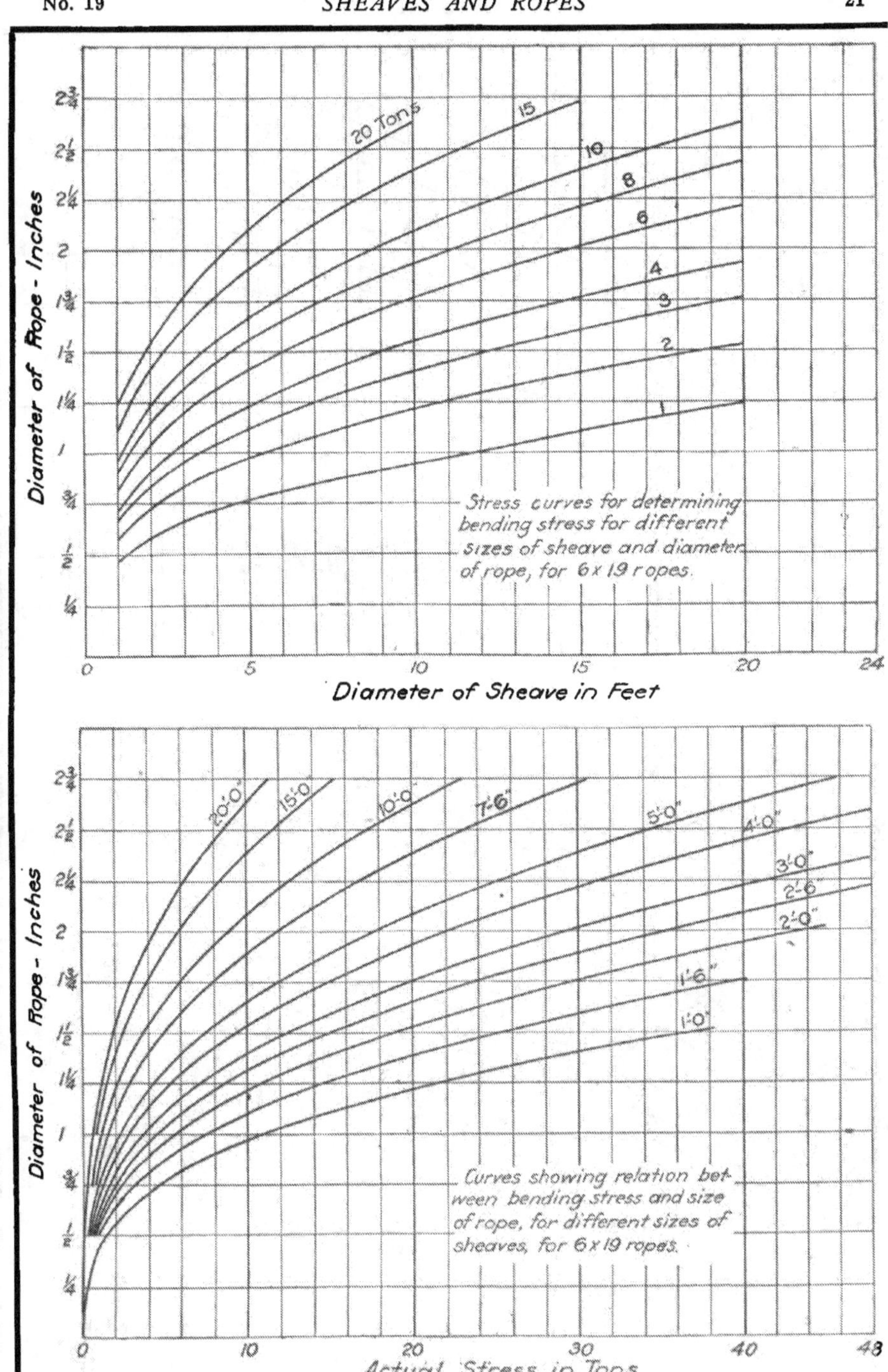
BENDING STRESSES IN WIRE ROPES—II
Diameter of Rope - Inches
20 Tons
15
10
8
6
4
3
2
1
Stress curves for determining
bending stress for different
sizes of sheave and diameter
of rope, for 6 x 19 ropes.
2¾
2½
2¼
2
1¾
1½
1¼
1
¾
½
¼
0   5   10   15   20   24
Diameter of Sheave in Feet
Diameter of Rope - Inches
20'-0"
15'-0"
10'-0"
7'-6"
5'-0"
4'-0"
3'-0"
2'-6"
2'-0"
1'-6"
1'-0"
Curves showing relation between bending stress and size
of rope, for different sizes of
sheaves, for 6 x 19 ropes.
2¾
2½
2¼
2
1¾
1½
1¼
1
¾
½
¼
0   10   20   30   40   48
Actual Stress in Tons

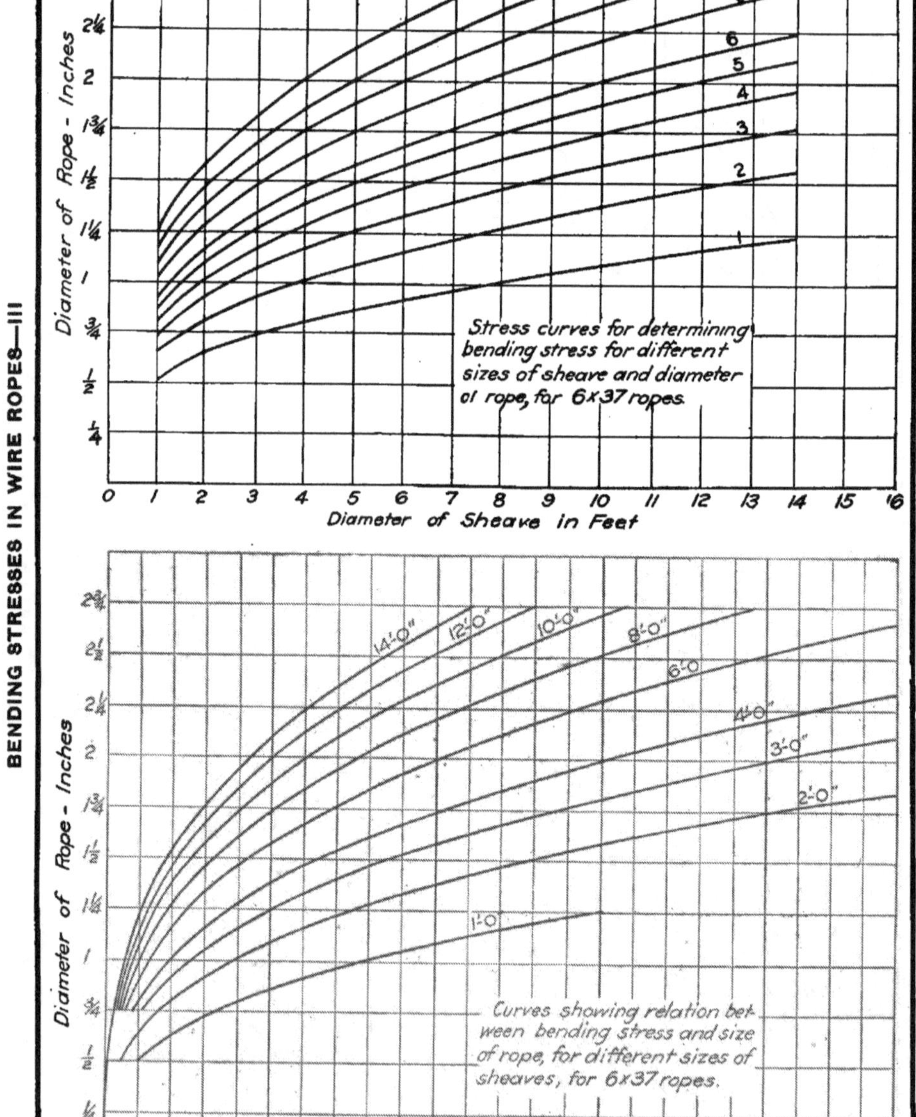
BENDING STRESSES IN WIRE ROPES—III

Diameter of Rope - Inches

15 Tons
12
10
8
6
5
4
3
2
1

Stress curves for determining
bending stress for different
sizes of sheave and diameter
of rope, for 6x37 ropes.

Diameter of Sheave in Feet

Diameter of Rope - Inches

14'-0"
12'-0"
10'-0"
8'-0"
6'-0"
4'-0"
3'-0"
2'-0"
1'-0"

Curves showing relation between bending stress and size
of rope, for different sizes of
sheaves, for 6x37 ropes.

Actual Stress in Tons

Contributed by James F. Howe, Machinery's Data Sheet No. 70. Explanatory note: Page 32.

BENDING STRESSES IN WIRE ROPES—IV

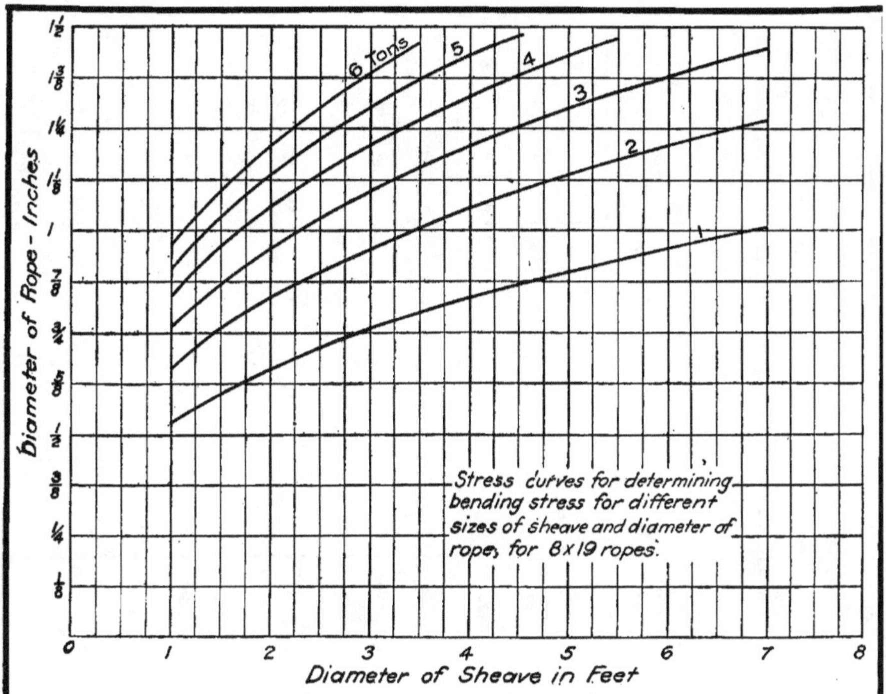

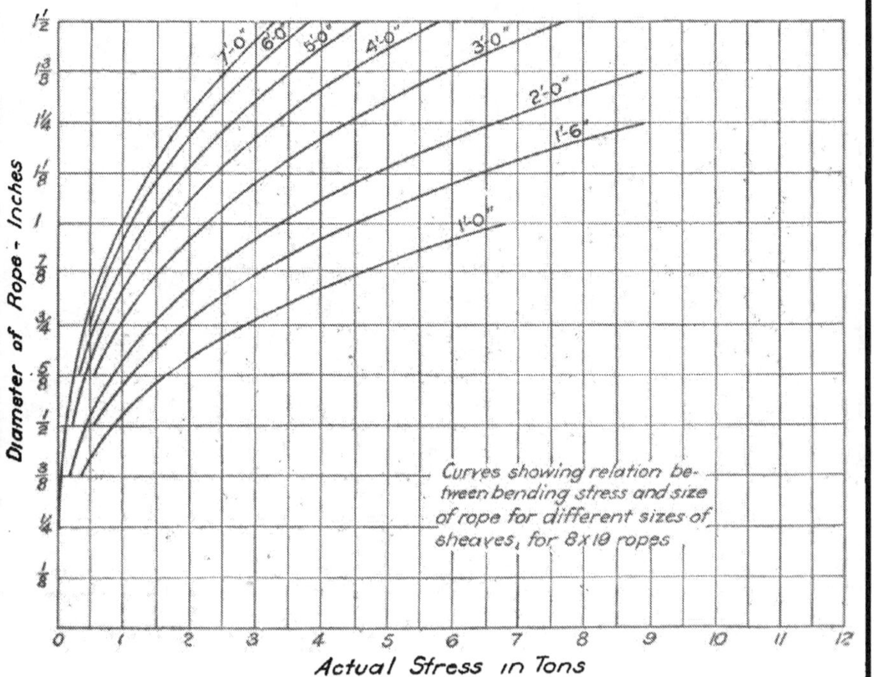

Diameter of Rope - Inches
6 Tons
5
4
3
2
1
Stress curves for determining
bending stress for different
sizes of sheave and diameter of
rope, for 8x19 ropes.
Diameter of Sheave in Feet
0   1   2   3   4   5   6   7   8

Diameter of Rope - Inches
7'-0"   6'-0"   5'-0"   4'-0"   3'-0"   2'-0"   1'-6"   1'-0"
Curves showing relation be-
tween bending stress and size
of rope for different sizes of
sheaves, for 8x19 ropes
Actual Stress in Tons
0   1   2   3   4   5   6   7   8   9   10   11   12

DIMENSIONS OF SPROCKET WHEEL TEETH FOR STANDARD DETACHABLE CHAIN

Standard of the C.O. Bartlett & Snow Co., Cleveland, Ohio.

All dimensions in inches.

No. of Sprocket or Chain	A	B	C	D	E	F	G	P	R	Sprockets Smallest Pitch Diam.	Sprockets No. Teeth
25	$\frac{1}{4}$	$\frac{13}{32}$	$\frac{3}{16}$	$\frac{7}{16}$	$\frac{3}{8}$	$\frac{3}{16}$	$\frac{1}{8}$	$\frac{7}{8}$	$\frac{1}{8}$	$1\frac{1}{2}$	5
32	$\frac{9}{32}$	$\frac{7}{16}$	$\frac{1}{4}$	$\frac{9}{16}$	$\frac{7}{16}$	$\frac{7}{32}$	$\frac{1}{8}$	$1\frac{1}{8}$	$\frac{1}{8}$	2	5
33	$\frac{7}{32}$	$\frac{15}{32}$	$\frac{7}{32}$	$\frac{11}{16}$	$\frac{1}{2}$	$\frac{1}{4}$	$\frac{1}{8}$	$1\frac{3}{8}$	$\frac{3}{16}$	$2\frac{3}{4}$	6
34	$\frac{7}{32}$	$\frac{15}{32}$	$\frac{7}{32}$	$\frac{11}{16}$	$\frac{1}{2}$	$\frac{1}{4}$	$\frac{1}{8}$	$1\frac{3}{8}$	$\frac{3}{16}$	$2\frac{3}{4}$	6
35	$\frac{7}{16}$	$\frac{5}{8}$	$\frac{5}{16}$	$\frac{11}{16}$	$\frac{9}{16}$	$\frac{9}{32}$	$\frac{1}{8}$	$1\frac{5}{8}$	$\frac{3}{16}$	$2\frac{1}{2}$	5
42	$\frac{11}{32}$	$\frac{19}{32}$	$\frac{9}{32}$	$\frac{5}{8}$	$\frac{1}{2}$	$\frac{1}{4}$	$\frac{1}{8}$	$1\frac{3}{8}$	$\frac{3}{16}$	2	5
45	$\frac{7}{16}$	$\frac{5}{8}$	$\frac{5}{16}$	$\frac{11}{16}$	$\frac{9}{16}$	$\frac{9}{32}$	$\frac{1}{8}$	$1\frac{5}{8}$	$\frac{3}{16}$	$2\frac{1}{2}$	5
51	$\frac{3}{8}$	$\frac{19}{32}$	$\frac{1}{4}$	$\frac{1}{2}$	$\frac{7}{16}$	$\frac{7}{32}$	$\frac{1}{8}$	$1\frac{1}{8}$	$\frac{3}{16}$	$1\frac{3}{4}$	5
52	$\frac{7}{16}$	$\frac{3}{4}$	$\frac{3}{8}$	$\frac{13}{16}$	$\frac{11}{16}$	$\frac{11}{32}$	$\frac{1}{8}$	$1\frac{1}{2}$	$\frac{1}{4}$	$2\frac{3}{4}$	6
$52\frac{1}{2}$	$\frac{7}{16}$	$\frac{3}{4}$	$\frac{3}{8}$	$\frac{13}{16}$	$\frac{11}{16}$	$\frac{11}{32}$	$\frac{1}{8}$	$1\frac{1}{2}$	$\frac{1}{4}$	$2\frac{3}{4}$	6

No. of Sprocket or Chain	A	B	C	D	E	F	G	P	R	Sprockets Smallest Pitch Diam.	Sprockets No. Teeth
55	$\frac{7}{16}$	$\frac{5}{8}$	$\frac{5}{16}$	$\frac{11}{16}$	$\frac{9}{16}$	$\frac{9}{32}$	$\frac{1}{8}$	$1\frac{5}{8}$	$\frac{3}{16}$	$2\frac{1}{2}$	5
57	$\frac{9}{16}$	$\frac{3}{4}$	$\frac{7}{16}$	1	$\frac{5}{8}$	$\frac{5}{16}$	$\frac{3}{8}$	$2\frac{1}{4}$	$\frac{3}{8}$	$4\frac{1}{2}$	5
62	$\frac{9}{16}$	$\frac{3}{4}$	$\frac{5}{16}$	$\frac{13}{16}$	$\frac{11}{16}$	$\frac{11}{32}$	$\frac{3}{16}$	$1\frac{5}{8}$	$\frac{3}{8}$	$3\frac{3}{4}$	7
66	$\frac{1}{2}$	$\frac{3}{4}$	$\frac{3}{8}$	$\frac{7}{8}$	$\frac{5}{8}$	$\frac{5}{16}$	$\frac{1}{4}$	2	$\frac{1}{4}$	5	8
67	$\frac{9}{16}$	$\frac{3}{4}$	$\frac{7}{16}$	1	$\frac{5}{8}$	$\frac{5}{16}$	$\frac{3}{8}$	$2\frac{1}{4}$	$\frac{3}{8}$	$4\frac{1}{2}$	5
75	$\frac{17}{32}$	$\frac{3}{4}$	$\frac{7}{16}$	$1\frac{5}{16}$	1	$\frac{1}{2}$	$\frac{3}{8}$	$2\frac{5}{8}$	$\frac{1}{2}$	$4\frac{1}{4}$	5
77	$\frac{9}{16}$	$\frac{3}{4}$	$\frac{7}{16}$	1	$\frac{5}{8}$	$\frac{5}{16}$	$\frac{3}{8}$	$2\frac{1}{4}$	$\frac{3}{8}$	$4\frac{1}{2}$	5
78	$\frac{17}{32}$	$\frac{3}{4}$	$\frac{7}{16}$	$1\frac{5}{16}$	1	$\frac{1}{2}$	$\frac{3}{8}$	$2\frac{5}{8}$	$\frac{1}{2}$	$4\frac{1}{4}$	5
85	$1\frac{13}{16}$	2	$\frac{7}{16}$	$1\frac{7}{16}$	$\frac{15}{16}$	$\frac{15}{32}$	—	$3\frac{7}{8}$	0	$7\frac{3}{4}$	6
88	$\frac{17}{32}$	$\frac{3}{4}$	$\frac{7}{16}$	$1\frac{5}{16}$	1	$\frac{1}{2}$	$\frac{3}{8}$	$2\frac{5}{8}$	$\frac{1}{2}$	$4\frac{1}{4}$	5
95	$1\frac{13}{16}$	2	$\frac{7}{16}$	$1\frac{7}{16}$	$\frac{15}{16}$	$\frac{15}{32}$	—	$3\frac{7}{8}$	0	$7\frac{3}{4}$	6
103	$\frac{13}{16}$	$1\frac{1}{8}$	$\frac{9}{16}$	$1\frac{9}{16}$	$1\frac{1}{4}$	$\frac{5}{8}$	$\frac{3}{8}$	$3\frac{1}{8}$	$\frac{1}{2}$	6	6
108	$2\frac{1}{4}$	$2\frac{1}{2}$	$\frac{7}{16}$	$1\frac{1}{2}$	$1\frac{1}{8}$	$\frac{9}{16}$	—	$4\frac{3}{4}$	0	$9\frac{1}{2}$	6
114	$\frac{15}{16}$	1	$\frac{7}{8}$	$1\frac{11}{16}$	$1\frac{1}{8}$	$\frac{9}{16}$	$\frac{1}{4}$	$3\frac{1}{4}$	$\frac{3}{8}$	7	7
124	$\frac{15}{16}$	$1\frac{1}{4}$	$\frac{3}{4}$	$2\frac{1}{8}$	$1\frac{1}{2}$	$\frac{3}{4}$	$\frac{1}{2}$	4	$\frac{3}{4}$	$9\frac{1}{2}$	7

Contributed by F. G. Walker, MACHINERY'S Data Sheet No. 108. Explanatory note: Page 32.

STANDARD SPROCKET WHEELS AND DETACHABLE CHAIN

Sprocket Wheels for Standard Detachable Chain.	Standard Detachable Chain. (Malleable Iron)					
	Number of Chain	Working Stress in Pounds	Approx. Links Per 10 Feet	Number of Chain	Working Stress in Pounds	Approx. Links Per 10 Feet
Standard sprocket wheels for detachable chain, work in either direction and are known by numbers, corresponding to the numbers of the standard detachable chain commonly called "Driving or Engineering Chain."	25	75	133	66	700	60
	32	150	104	67	700	52
Standard Bores for Detachable Chain Sprocket Wheels.	33	200	86	75	750	46
Standard Sprocket Wheel No. 25, 32, 33, 34 Bore, $1\frac{7}{16}''$	34	225	86	77	800	52
" " " " 42 " $1\frac{11}{16}''$	35	250	74	78	1000	46
" " " " 35, 45, 51, 52, 52½, 55 " $1\frac{15}{32}''$	42	300	88	85	1300	30
" " " " 57, 62, 66, 67, 77 " $2\frac{7}{16}''$	45	350	74	88	1200	46
" " " " 75, 78, 85, 88, 95 " $2\frac{15}{16}''$	51	375	104	95	1600	30
" " " " 103, 108, 114 " $3\frac{7}{16}''$	52	400	80	103	1800	39
" " " " 124 " $3\frac{15}{16}''$	52½	450	80	108	1800	25
No. 33 and 34 Chain works on the same sprocket wheels.	55	450	74	114	2000	36
No. 35, 45 and 55 " " " " " " "	57	600	52	124	2250	30
No. 52 and 52½ " " " " " " "	62	650	73			
No. 57, 67 and 77 " " " " " " "						
No. 75, 78 and 88 " " " " " " "	The chain is interchangeable with all standard link belting, and works upon standard sprocket wheels of corresponding numbers.					
No. 85 and 95 " " " " " " "						

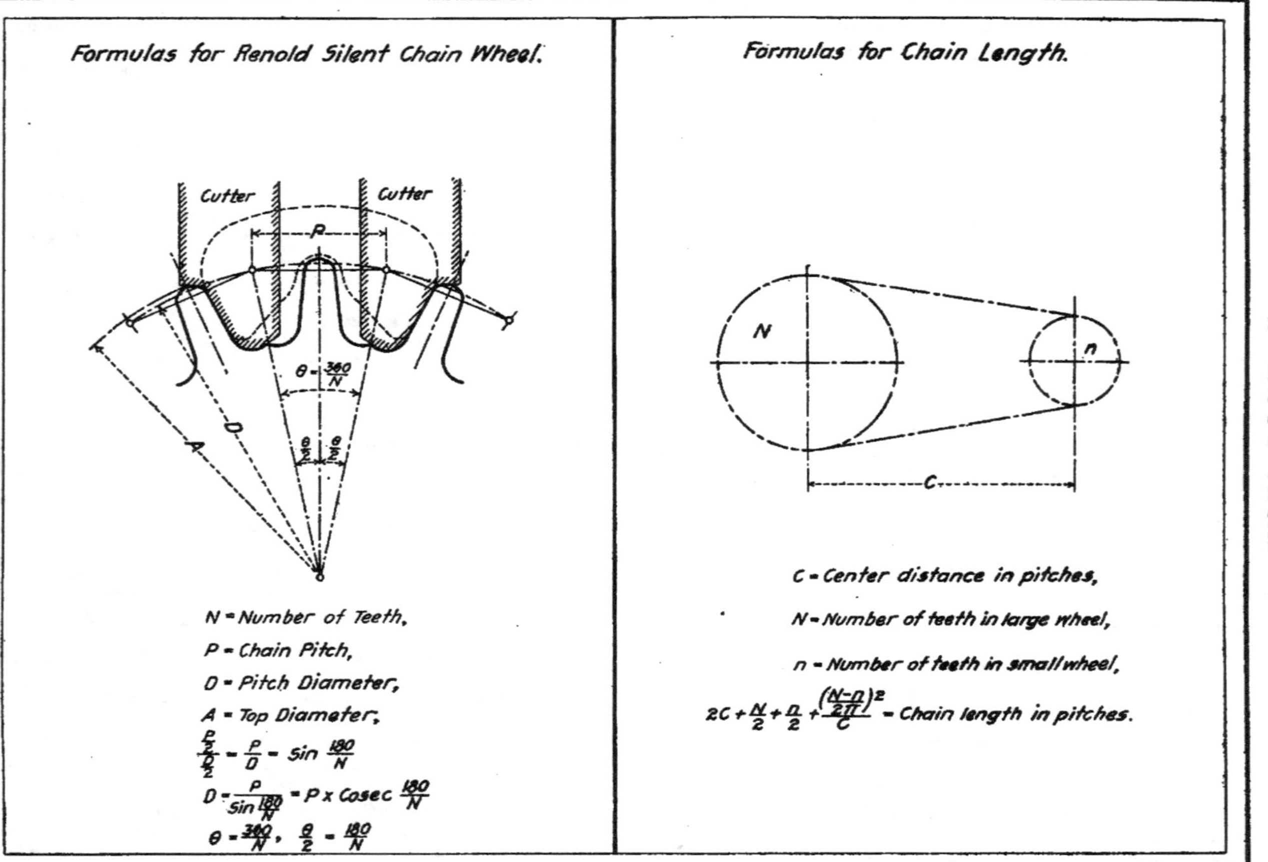

$$\frac{P}{2} = \frac{P}{D} = \sin\frac{180}{N}$$

$$D = \frac{P}{\sin\frac{180}{N}} = P \times \operatorname{Cosec}\frac{180}{N}$$

$$\theta = \frac{360}{N}, \quad \frac{\theta}{2} = \frac{180}{N}$$

$$2C + \frac{N}{2} + \frac{n}{2} + \frac{\left(\frac{N-n}{2\pi}\right)^2}{C} = \text{Chain length in pitches.}$$

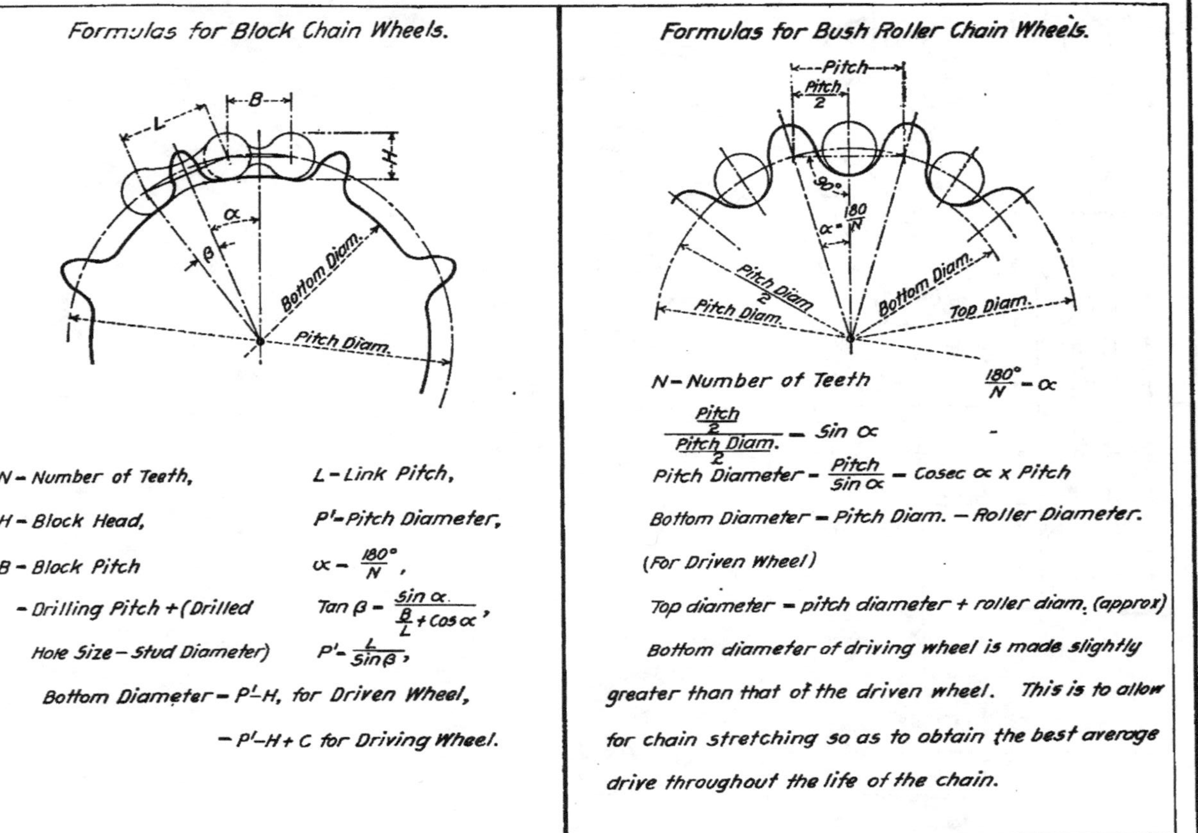

Formulas for Block Chain Wheels.

N — Number of Teeth,

H — Block Head,

B — Block Pitch

— Drilling Pitch + (Drilled

Hole Size — Stud Diameter)

L — Link Pitch,

P¹ — Pitch Diameter,

$\alpha = \dfrac{180°}{N}$,

$\text{Tan } \beta = \dfrac{\sin\alpha}{\dfrac{B}{L} + \cos\alpha}$,

$P^1 = \dfrac{L}{\sin\beta}$,

Bottom Diameter $= P^1{-}H$, for Driven Wheel,

$\qquad = P^1{-}H + C$ for Driving Wheel.

Formulas for Bush Roller Chain Wheels.

N — Number of Teeth

$\dfrac{\dfrac{Pitch}{2}}{\dfrac{Pitch\ Diam.}{2}} = \sin\alpha$

$\dfrac{180°}{N} = \alpha$

Pitch Diameter $= \dfrac{Pitch}{\sin\alpha} = \text{Cosec }\alpha \times Pitch$

Bottom Diameter = Pitch Diam. — Roller Diameter.

(For Driven Wheel)

Top diameter = pitch diameter + roller diam. (approx)

Bottom diameter of driving wheel is made slightly greater than that of the driven wheel. This is to allow for chain stretching so as to obtain the best average drive throughout the life of the chain.

SPROCKET WHEELS FOR ORDINARY LINK CHAIN—I

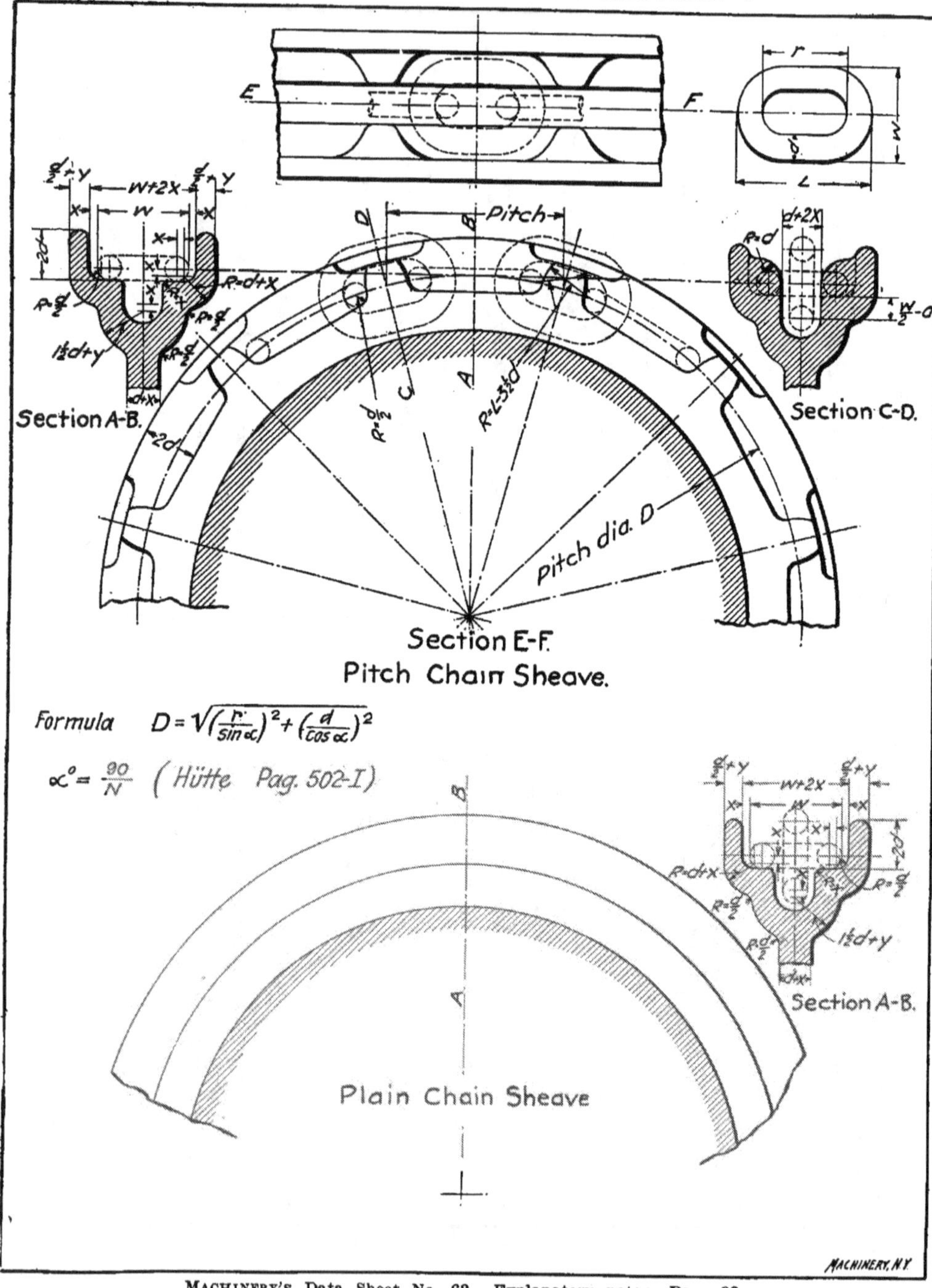

Formula $\quad D = \sqrt{\left(\dfrac{r}{\sin\alpha}\right)^2 + \left(\dfrac{d}{\cos\alpha}\right)^2}$

$\alpha^\circ = \dfrac{90}{N}$ (Hütte Pag. 502-I)

SPROCKET WHEELS FOR ORDINARY LINK CHAIN—II

No of Teeth = N =			5	6	7	8	9	10	11	12	13	14	15	16	17		
Angle α° =			18°0'	15°0'	12°51.4'	11°15'	10°0'	9°0'	8°10.9'	7°30'	6°55.4'	6°25.7'	6°0'	5°37.5'	5°17.64'		
d= size of chain	L= length of link	W= width of link	D= Pitch Diameter														X	Y
3/16"	1 3/8"	13/16"	3.24	3.87	4.50	5.13	5.76	6.40	7.03	7.66	8.29	8.93	9.57	10.20	10.84	1/16"	3/32"
1/4"	1 1/2"	1"	3.25	3.87	4.50	5.13	5.76	6.40	7.03	7.66	8.29	8.93	9.57	10.20	10.84	3/32"	3/32"
5/16"	1 3/4"	1 3/16"	3.65	4.35	5.06	5.77	6.48	7.18	7.91	8.62	9.33	10.05	10.76	11.47	12.19	3/32"	3/32"
3/8"	2"	1 3/8"	4.06	4.85	5.63	6.42	7.21	8.00	8.79	9.59	10.38	11.17	11.96	12.76	13.56	3/32"	3/32"
7/16"	2 1/4"	1 9/16"	4.49	5.31	6.18	7.06	7.74	8.79	9.67	10.53	11.41	12.28	13.16	14.03	14.90	3/32"	3/32"
1/2"	2 1/2"	1 3/4"	4.86	5.80	6.76	7.71	8.65	9.61	10.55	11.49	12.45	13.40	14.35	15.30	16.26	3/32"	1/16"
9/16"	2 7/8"	1 15/16"	5.69	6.79	7.88	8.97	10.08	11.19	12.30	13.41	14.52	15.63	16.74	17.85	18.97	1/8"	1/16"
5/8"	3 1/4"	2 1/8"	6.51	7.75	9.01	10.27	11.53	12.80	14.07	15.33	16.60	17.90	19.14	20.41	21.68	1/8"	1/16"
11/16"	3 1/2"	2 5/16"	6.91	8.25	9.58	10.91	12.26	13.61	14.95	16.29	17.65	18.99	20.34	21.69	23.04	1/8"	1/16"
3/4"	3 3/4"	2 1/2"	7.32	8.73	10.14	11.56	12.98	14.40	15.83	17.26	18.68	20.06	21.54	22.97	24.40	1/8"	1/16"
13/16"	4"	2 11/16"	7.73	9.21	10.71	12.20	13.72	15.21	16.71	18.20	19.72	21.23	22.74	24.24	25.75	1/8"	1/16"
7/8"	4 1/4"	3"	8.17	9.70	11.27	12.85	14.43	16.01	17.55	19.17	20.76	22.35	23.93	25.52	27.11	1/8"	1/16"
15/16"	4 1/2"	3 1/4"	8.55	10.19	11.84	13.50	15.15	16.81	18.47	20.13	21.80	23.46	25.13	26.80	28.47	1/8"	1/16"
1"	4 3/4"	3 1/2"	8.96	10.68	12.40	14.13	15.87	17.61	19.35	21.09	22.84	24.58	26.33	28.08	29.83	1/8"	
1 1/8"	5 1/2"	3 7/8"	10.58	12.61	14.66	16.71	18.76	20.81	22.87	24.93	26.99	29.05	31.11	33.18	35.25	1/8"	
1 1/4"	6"	4 1/4"	11.40	13.58	15.78	17.99	20.20	22.41	24.63	26.84	29.06	31.28	33.51	35.73	37.95	5/32"	
1 3/8"	6 1/2"	4 3/4"	12.22	14.56	16.91	19.27	21.64	24.01	26.39	28.75	31.14	33.52	35.90	38.37	40.67	5/32"	
1 1/2"	7 1/4"	5 1/4"	13.85	16.49	19.16	21.84	24.52	27.21	29.91	32.52	35.29	37.99	40.69			5/32"	
1 5/8"	7 7/8"	5 3/4"	15.06	17.95	20.85	23.77	26.62	29.61	32.54	35.47	38.41	41.34				5/32"	

SPROCKET WHEELS FOR ORDINARY LINK CHAIN—III

No. of Teeth = N =			18	19	20	21	22	23	24	25	26	27	28	29	30		
Angle α° =			5°0'	4°44.22'	4°30'	4°17.14'	4°5.45'	3°54.78'	3°45'	3°36'	3°27.69'	3°20'	3°12.85'	3°6.18'	3°0'		
d = size of chain	l = length of link	w = width of link	D = Pitch Diameter													X	Y
3/16"	1 3/8"	13/16"	11.47	12.11	12.75	13.38	14.02	14.66	15.29	15.93	16.56	17.20	17.84	18.47	19.11	1/16"	3/32"
1/4"	1 1/2"	1"	11.47	12.11	12.75	13.38	14.02	14.66	15.29	15.93	16.56	17.20	17.84	18.47	19.11	3/32"	3/32"
5/16"	1 3/4"	1 3/16"	12.91	13.62	14.34	15.05	15.77	16.49	17.20	17.92	18.62	19.34	20.06	20.80	21.50	3/32"	3/32"
3/8"	2"	1 3/8"	14.36	15.16	15.96	16.74	17.53	18.32	19.11	19.90	20.70	21.50	22.29	23.08	23.88	3/32"	3/32"
7/16"	2 1/4"	1 9/16"	15.78	16.65	17.53	18.40	19.27	20.15	21.02	21.90	22.77	23.65	24.52	25.40	26.27	3/32"	3/32"
1/2"	2 1/2"	1 3/4"	17.21	18.16	19.12	20.07	21.03	21.98	22.94	23.89	24.85	25.80	26.75	27.71	28.66	3/32"	1/16"
9/16"	2 7/8"	1 15/16"	20.08	21.19	22.30	23.42	24.53	25.64	26.76	27.87	28.98	30.10	31.21	32.32	33.43	1/8"	1/16"
5/8"	3 1/4"	2 1/8"	22.95	24.22	25.50	26.77	28.03	29.31	30.58	31.85	33.13	34.40	35.67	36.94	38.25	1/8"	1/16"
11/16"	3 1/2"	2 5/16"	24.34	25.73	27.09	28.44	29.79	31.14	32.49	33.84	35.20	36.55	37.90	39.25	40.60	1/8"	1/16"
3/4"	3 3/4"	2 1/2"	25.83	27.26	28.69	30.12	31.55	32.97	34.41	35.84	37.27	38.70	40.04			1/8"	1/16"
13/16"	4"	2 11/16"	27.26	28.77	30.28	31.79	33.30	34.81	36.32	37.83	39.34	40.85				1/8"	1/16"
7/8"	4 1/4"	3"	28.70	30.29	31.88	33.46	35.04	36.63	38.23	39.82	41.41					1/8"	1/16"
15/16"	4 1/2"	3 1/4"	30.14	31.80	33.46	35.13	36.83	38.48	40.15							1/8"	1/16"
1"	4 3/4"	3 1/2"	31.57	33.31	35.06	36.81	38.56	40.30								1/8"	
1 1/8"	5 1/2"	3 7/8"	37.32	39.38	41.45											1/8"	
1 1/4"	6"	4 1/4"	40.18													5/32"	
1 3/8"	6 1/2"	4 3/4"														5/32"	
1 1/2"	7 1/4"	5 1/4"														5/32"	
1 5/8"	7 7/8"	5 3/4"														5/32"	

HORSEPOWER TRANSMITTED BY CHAIN DRIVES

This Table gives values for ideal conditions. For ordinary duty deduct from 30 to 40 per cent.

Detachable Link Belt				Jeffrey Meg-Oborn Chain			
Trade No.	Working Strain, Pounds	Horsepower		Trade No.	Working Strain, Pounds	Horsepower	
		250 Feet	500 Feet			250 Feet	500 Feet
25	75	0.56	1.12	25	100	0.75	1.50
32	150	1.12	2.25	—	—	—	—
33	200	1.50	3.00	33	250	1.12	2.25
34	225	1.68	3.37	34	250	1.12	2.25
35	250	1.87	3.75	—	—	—	—
42	300	2.25	4.50	42	400	3.00	6.00
45	350	2.50	5.02	45	400	3.00	6.00
51	375	2.81	5.62	50	250	1.12	2.25
52	500	3.75	7.50	52	600	4.50	9.00
52½-55	450	3.37	6.75	55	600	4.50	9.00
57	600	4.50	9.00	52 spec.	800	6.00	12.00
62	650	4.87	9.75	57	700	5.25	10.50
66-67	700	5.25	10.50	62-67	750	5.62	11.25
75	750	5.62	11.25	75	1000	7.50	15.00
77	800	6.00	12.00	77	900	6.75	13.50
78	1000	7.50	15.00	78	1100	8.25	16.50
83-88	1200	9.00	18.00	83	1500	11.12	22.25
85	1300	9.75	19.50	85	1600	12.00	24.00
95	1600	12.00	24.00	88	1300	9.75	19.50
103-108	1800	13.50	27.00	103-121	2000	15.00	30.00
114	2000	15.00	30.00	108	2200	16.50	33.00
104½	2100	15.75	31.50	122-146	3000	22.50	45.00
122	2200	16.50	33.00	124	4000	30.00	60.00
124	2250	16.87	33.75	—	—	—	—

To find H.P. at any other speed up to 1000 feet per minute, proceed thus: Find H.P. in table for chain at 500 feet. Then multiply this H.P. by speed required and divide result by 500. Example: Required H.P. of M.O. chain No. 124 at 700 feet. Capacity of No. 124 M.O. chain at 500 feet = 60 H.P. Then 60 × 700 ÷ 500 = 84 H.P. at 700 feet.

of the column containing 1100, and in this case equals 150 revolutions per minute. [MACHINERY'S Reference Series No. 18, Shop Arithmetic for the Machinist, third edition, Chapter VII, Speed of Pulleys.]

Horsepower Transmitted by Belting

On pages 14 and 15 two tables are given by means of which the horsepower transmitted by belting may be found. In the table on page 14 the horsepower transmitted is given directly, this table being used by a concern making a specialty of belt transmissions and pulleys. On page 15, a table of constants is given by means of which the horsepower transmitted by belting or the width of belt required for transmitting a given horsepower may be found. This table is prepared from data given in an article entitled "Belt Factors," published in the *Journal of the Worcester Polytechnic Institute*, by Prof. William W. Bird, of the Worcester Polytechnic Institute.

On page 16 the horsepower transmitted by manila rope is given. In preparing this table the effect of centrifugal force has been taken into account. The table has not been carried up to a rope velocity of more than 7500 feet per minute, because it is impractical to run ropes at a higher speed. [MACHINERY, April, 1899, Rules for Determining the Horsepower of Belts; July and August, 1901, Power Transmission by Belts; July, 1906, Horsepower Transmitted by Belts; September, 1906, Horsepower Transmitted by Leather Belts per Inch of Width; August, 1909, The Transmission of Power by Ropes; MACHINERY'S Reference Series No. 52, Advanced Shop Arithmetic for the Machinist, Chapter VI, Horsepower of Belting.]

Sheaves for Ropes

On page 17 a table is given for proportioning sheaves for iron and steel ropes, and on pages 18 and 19, tables for the grooves in regular and idler sheaves for manila ropes. These tables are based upon approved current practice. [MACHINERY, December, 1 9 0 9, Sheaves for Manila Rope.]

Bending Stresses in Wire Ropes

On pages 20 to 23, inclusive, diagrams are given for determining the stresses occurring in wire ropes due to bending them over sheaves of different diameters. Assume that a one-inch rope is bent over a sheave 11 feet in diameter. From page 20 we find by locating the sheave diameter on the bottom scale of the upper diagram, and the diameter of the rope on the left-hand scale and following the vertical and horizontal lines from the points so located until they intersect, that the stress in the rope due to the bending is two tons, as indicated by the curve passing through the point of intersection. The different diagrams refer to ropes of different construction. On each page the curves in the upper diagram give tons stress, and the curves in the lower diagram give the diameter of pulley, so that the third factor can conveniently be found when any two factors are known. The example given illustrates the use of the various diagrams. [MACHINERY, June, 1907, Bending Stresses in Wire Rope; February, 1909, Stresses in Wire Ropes Due to Bending; MACHINERY'S Reference Series No. 24, Examples of Calculating Designs, Chapter III, Bending Stresses in Wire Rope.]

Chains and Chain Drive

On pages 24 to 30, inclusive, are given dimensions for sprockets and chains of different types, including formulas for Renold chain and for block and roller chain sprockets. On page 31, tables of the horsepower which can be transmitted by detachable link belt and by the Jeffrey Mey-Oborn chain are given. [MACHINERY, February, 1905, Roller Chain Power Transmission and Construction of Sprockets; February, 1909, Chain Drives.]